AUTOMOTI

GW00374938

AUTOMOTIVE GLASSFIBRE

A PRACTICAL GUIDE TO MOULDING AND REPAIR

DENNIS FOY

MOTOR RACING PUBLICATIONS LTD
Unit 6, The Pilton Estate, 46 Pitlake,
Croydon CR0 3RY, England

First published 1987
This edition 1995

**British Library Cataloguing-in-Publication Data.
A catalogue record for this book is available from
the British Library.**

ISBN 1 899870 04 0

**Whilst every care has been taken to ensure the
correctness of the information in this book, neither
the author nor the publishers can accept any
liability for loss, damage or injury resulting from
errors or omissions.**

Printed in Great Britain by
The Amadeus Press Ltd, Huddersfield, West Yorkshire

CONTENTS

ABOUT THE AUTHOR

Dennis Foy was born in Warrington, Cheshire, and seems to have spent most of his life in the magnetic world of cars and motorcycles — building them, modifying them, competing in them, and writing about them.

A professional journalist since the late seventies, Dennis had a four-year stint as Features Editor of *Hot Car* magazine, followed by a return to a freelance existence writing books and magazine features. His first book *Escort Performance* was published by Motor Racing Publications in 1984 then revised and expanded in 1994. In 1987, his wife and he created *Performance Ford* magazine, which has become one of the biggest one-marque titles on the British Market. A member of the Institute of the Motor Industry, he lives happily with his wife Pat and son Ben in their native Cheshire.

THE WITHOUT WHOMS

There are a number of people who have helped out during the long gestation period of this book, and without whose help it would never have made it into print.

The first of these is Ian Franz, a man with an unrivalled knowledge of practical glassfibre lamination. Had it not been for his (mostly) patient tuition in the craft over a long period of time at his workshops, I would know nothing of the subject. In addition to the practical guidance, Ian gave me a vast amount of time discussing the theory of the subject, and subsequently help revising the early drafts of the manuscript. He and his wife May have been great and valued friends to my wife and me for some years, and we appreciate it.

Then there were people such as Jeremy Snook of Porsche Cars GB, Wayne Cherry of Vauxhall Motors, Noel Palmer of TVR, Ken Stanley of Bighead Fasteners, Mr Thurman of BIP, and the staff at Strand Glassfibre in Stockport, all of whom have assisted with either information or photographs of their products.

Most of all, though, thanks go to my wife Pat, for her encouragement and patience during the two years it took to put this book together. Without her help, the manuscript would never have seen the light of day . . . .

Dennis Foy

INTRODUCTION

Glassfibre lamination has to be one of the most objectionable jobs to be found within the automotive industry; it is dirty, smelly, can ruin the skin, injure the eyes and lungs, and wrecks clothes, equipment and facilities at an alarming rate. Yet for modifying body-work and for producing one-off panels, it offers an unrivalled degree of flexibility and durability.

What I have set out to do in this book is to show just how useful the process can be, and at the same time give ways of keeping its anti-social aspects to a minimum — and that includes the cost factor.

It is easy to go wrong when using glassfibre products, and where most amateurs seem to slip up is by failing to understand the complexities of the materials involved. For instance, if you were to ask anybody about to undertake a lamination project to list the materials that they will be using, the answer is almost invariably that they will be buying resin, catalyst and matting. But did you know that there are a number of different resin types available, all of which have peculiar characteristics and specific applications? That there are a number of different weights of matting to be had, and that there are products such as woven rovings which can, on occasion, be far more suitable than matting? In order to clarify matters, I have detailed the range of generally-available

By far the widest single market for glassfibre is the kit car industry. This is one of the highest-standard kits available, the GTD 40.

materials, and made an attempt to translate obscure technical data into easily-understood English.

Having the right environment in which to work is another step closer to success, and for that reason I have given advice on setting up a suitable workshop. Similarly, I discovered some time ago that it is essential to have the right range of tools and equipment available — the strictly-limited time confines of the materials often means that there is no room for bodging — and so I have looked to suggesting throughout each of the

Whilst Lotus have gone over to state-of-the-art composite laminations and injection-moulding techniques, TVR prefer to keep to hand-laid glassfibre for their excellent bodyshells.

A laminator at work in TVR's Blackpool factory. The bonnet for one of the Fylde Fliers is being laid up.

projects just what hardware will be needed to complete the exercise successfully.

In the projects themselves, I have endeavoured to cover each main area of modifying, repairing or moulding in glassfibre, and treated each exercise as self-contained. For this reason, there is a degree of repeating myself throughout that section of the book. The reason behind this is that you may well wish to have the book in the workshop with you as you produce your masterpiece — and constant cross-reference to different chapters would, under those circumstances, be nothing short of a pain.

Wherever possible, I have included any practical short cuts, and on occasion these may appear a shade unorthodox. Experience, however, has proved them to work. One or two of them may elicit a wince or a sharp intake of breath from a professional laminator — but don't let that put you off. This book is not aimed at the professional but at the enthusiastic amateur who, like me, can on a bad day have two left hands full of thumbs.

The author (left) with mentor Ian Franz. Photograph taken during assembly of Ian's Marina drag race car, which featured, naturally enough, abundant use of lightweight glassfibre panels.

I will finish this introduction with a cautionary note; before going anywhere near any materials, read and memorize the contents of the chapter on safety, Chapter 14. By doing so, you will be availing yourself of the knowledge necessary to overcome any potentially dangerous situations, and also become informed of what to do should the worst happen, and an accident befall you.

I hope that you find the book useful.

Cheshire, 1986   Dennis Foy

PART 1

WORKSHOP
AND
EQUIPMENT

CHAPTER 1

A PLACE TO WORK

Having the right environment in which to produce glassfibre laminations is essential. To achieve success, it is worthwhile spending a little time and money organizing a working area before you make a start on laying up any mouldings.

Firstly, it is necessary to have the workshop warm and dry — the simplest comparison that I can draw is with the inside of the average house on a typically nice spring day. If the workshop is too cool, or has too much moisture in its atmosphere, not only will the panels produced take substantially longer to cure, but there can also be problems such as air bubbles or gel-coat wrinkle appearing at a later date.

Of the various options available for heating a workshop, the best is a static radiator running from the domestic central heating system. Should you be planning to work in your garage and it happens to be attached to the house, the addition of another radiator (which can be turned off when not required) may be a worthwhile move, and not a particularly expensive one either — a secondhand dual radiator will only cost a tenner if you keep a close eye on the small ads in your local paper.

Should that ideal be beyond your means or capabilities, there are other options: a fan heater, a forced-air space heater, or the good old paraffin heater. Each has its

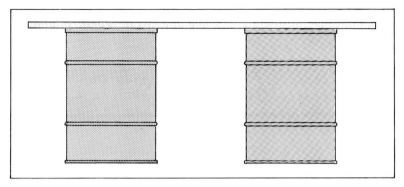

Whilst you couldn't call it 'high-tech', a combination of empty oil drums and sheets of laminated chipboard makes an excellent (and cheap) flexible bench system.

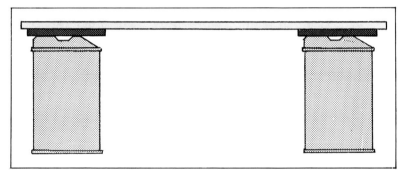

For a lower bench, use empty 5-gallon containers with a sheet of laminated board on top. Again, the cost is nominal. Contact a local garage for the empty drums.

advantages and disadvantages; paraffin and space heaters both work on the principle of a naked flame as heat source, which can be extremely dangerous given the highly-inflammable characteristics of some of the materials used in glassfibre lamination. Space heaters and fan heaters share a characteristic, too, in that they both circulate their heat by blowing air through the environment — meaning that dust flies when they are switched on. And that dust will land on wet resin with a casually-confident efficiency. All three types of heater, however, are very good at heating a workshop area quickly and economically.

In view of the shortcomings of the three types of heater, it follows that all three should be switched off before work begins, having first raised the temperature of the workshop to a reasonable degree. Or about 68 degrees (68°F or 20°C), to be more precise. A paraffin heater can be relit once lamination has been completed, but the other two types should be left off until the resin has cured to the 'green' stage.

Burning paraffin has one other unfortunate side-effect in that it releases quite large quantities of water vapour into the surrounding atmosphere. The resultant humidity could cause problems and will certainly tend to produce condensation on windows or any other cool surfaces, so it is very important to ensure adequate ventilation to change the air in the workshop if this form of heating is used.

Besides the problems of heating and humidity control, there are other aspects of equipping a workshop which must be considered before work begins.

The materials used are messy, which means that the walls and floor of the workshop should be treated in a manner which will make them easier to clean than they might otherwise be. Taking walls first, the ideal product that I have found for this application is heavy polythene sheet, which can be bought quite cheaply in roll form. The best place to source this is good old *Exchange & Mart,* closely followed by the 'Industrial Materials' column of the classified ads in the local newspaper. The beauty of this material is that once it gets intolerably dirty, it can be torn down and replaced without breaking the bank.

Should you be planning to do a lot of laminating, you may consider it worthwhile to go to the extravagant lengths of lining the workshop walls with laminate board of the Contiplas type. This material offers a neat and tidy finish, from which blobs of resin can be easily removed — especially if you go to the trouble of waxing the surface before work begins.

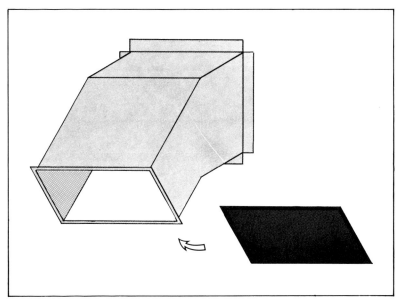

A vent shroud such as this can be made simply and quickly from glassfibre sheet. The filter is made from stretched net curtaining across a frame which affixes to the front of the duct.

The treatment that the workshop floor should receive will depend entirely upon its construction; a tarmac or concrete floor can be painted with a proprietary floor coating such as that produced by Evode, which can be periodically scraped and repainted. A wooden floor can be either gloss-painted, or covered with a cheap (and thus disposable) lino-type covering. The ultimate floor covering for a glassfibre workshop has to be ceramic tiles, but to use these would be so extravagant as to be totally decadent.

To be able to work on a variety of different mouldings, some kind of flexible work-bench arrangement is required, and the best thing that I have ever come across for this is a combination of (empty) 50-gallon oil drums, 5-gallon resin drums, and a selection of smooth boards. The oil drums are stood on end, with a board across the top, to form a bench at about waist height. The smaller drums, again topped off with a board, will give a lower

A bench such as this is ideal for mixing resin and so on. It may not look pretty after the years of service that it has seen, but it is very effective.

bench for use with higher jobs. Once again, the ideal boards are of the Contiplas variety, covered with a laminate surface which will be easy to clean off between jobs. For purposes of rigidity, I would recommend that the boards are at least 19mm thick.

Whilst not absolutely essential, the addition of some form of air extraction system which will draw out resin

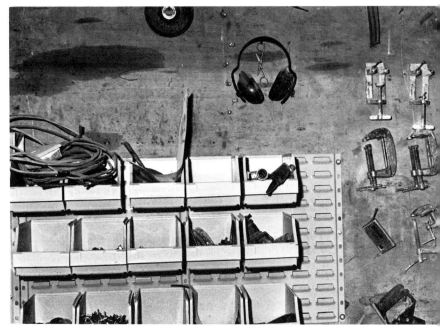

A sheet of board attached to the workshop wall will take hooks (or nails) from which to hang clamps and other tools as well as storage trays for 'odds & sods'.

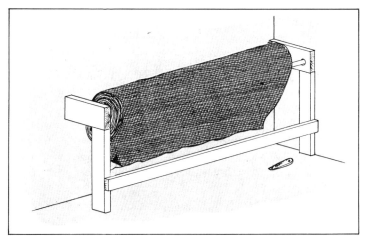

Should you use large quantities of matting, it would be worthwhile making a frame from timber to carry the roll. When not working, throw an old sheet across the matting to protect it from dust.

fumes and dust can make the working environment within a workshop far more healthy and comfortable. A domestic Vent-Axia or Xpelair will generally be quite adequate for this purpose. In order to minimize discomfort to your neighbours, it is advisable to incorporate some kind of ducting on the outside of the fan which will ensure that the roses next door don't get covered in dust — such flowers don't like that sort of treatment, and giving your neighbour a bedful of late Floribundae is hardly the best way to stay on good terms. With a little ingenuity, it is easy to make up a cowling with a mesh filter to trap the worst of the dust.

The final area of a workshop which should be given close attention is that for storing and mixing materials. As resins are at their best when stored at room temperature, these should be kept in the workshop. A system of shelves at convenient heights (remote from any direct heat source and out of the reach of inquisitive children, naturally) will suffice for storage, and a permanent bench against a wall, and convenient for the work area, will do nicely for mixing the resin and catalyst on. Another bench should be erected, this time for preparation of matting, rovings, etc. This bench should be kept clean and dry at all times.

How you store matting and roving depends upon the quantities you have 'in stock' at any given time; small pieces can be stored on a shelf, covered with a sheet of polythene to protect against dust, whilst rolls are best kept suspended, rather like kitchen rolls. A suitable roll holder is easily knocked together. Once again, cover the roll with a sheet of polythene when not in use — dusty matting can give rise to problems later.

CHAPTER 2

TOOLS FOR THE JOB

The first on the list of tools for use in glassfibre lamination is the paintbrush. A range of three sizes (one, two and four inch width) should suffice for just about every lamination job that you are likely to undertake, and these need not be particularly expensive brushes, as once they have been used for laminating, they are useless for any other purpose.

The brushes must be thoroughly cleaned out between jobs or mixes, using either a proprietary brush cleaner such as that sold by Strand Glassfibre, or, ideally, pure acetone. It is absolutely essential that they are dry and totally free of all traces of solvent before being used again, as even the merest hint of acetone will lead to severe problems such as gel-coat wrinkle or resin separation during the lamination process.

To assist the drainage of solvent, start by punching a hole through each side of the metal retaining ferrule. One hefty swipe with a hammer onto a strategically-positioned screwdriver will do the job nicely, thank you.

Once the brush has been immersed in solvent and worked through until all traces of resin have been removed from the bristles, wring out the brush and shake it out onto the ground; this will dispose of 90% of the acetone. To purge the remaining 10%, flick the brush back and forth across a convenient post or

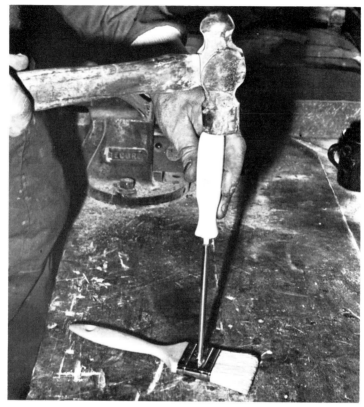

Tapping a hole into the side of the ferrule on a new paintbrush will aid the process of draining off acetone after cleaning the brush. Repeat the process on the other side of the brush.

Having a potful of acetone (which is covered with a lid, most of the time) on the bench aids the cleaning process — soak the tools in it as a preliminary to thorough washing out.

drainpipe, until all of the bristles are dry.

For applying resin to large areas, a lambswool roller is the ideal tool to use. Do not, however, be tempted to buy these from your local DIY store; those from such establishments are designed for use with emulsion paint, and come with plastic end-bearings which will vaporize before your very eyes as soon as they get so much as a whiff of acetone. Instead, buy a purpose-designed roller from your local glassfibre materials supplier. This will be fitted with bushes which are solvent-proof.

As with the paintbrushes, the roller must be completely clear of all traces of resin before it goes anywhere near another mix of resin. This is easiest to achieve by stripping the roller down, washing the handle and shaft assembly in acetone, and then washing the roller itself in

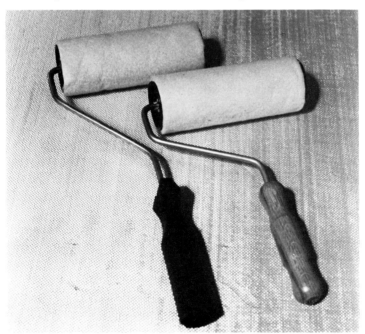

For laying up larger areas of glassfibre, use a paint roller. These should be bought from a specialist supplier, as ordinary DIY-store items may not be proof against the ravages of resin and acetone, and, if not, will disappear before your very eyes.

A selection of paintbrushes should be kept to hand. These five vary from 4in to ½in and will cater for most jobs between them.

another bowl of solvent. Once clean, shake off the excess acetone from the components, reassemble the tool, and run the roller quickly along a smooth, clean surface. And be prepared to be showered in a mist of acetone.

In order to extract air bubbles from a moulding, it is advisable, and often necessary, to use a metal roller. These are generally available in two designs, one of which uses equally-spaced metal washers along a shaft and is known as a disc roller. The other type has a roller with aluminium fluting along its length, and this is known as a paddle roller. Both are available in a variety of sizes, ranging from one to nine inches. Of the two types the paddle roller is the more widely used, and viewed by most laminators as the most efficient. Once again, cleanliness and a total freedom from acetone droplets are essential to successful usage.

Those three items are the main tools for laminating, and as you will gather, the costs involved are really quite modest. Where expense really starts to mount up is on the finishing side of the lamination process.

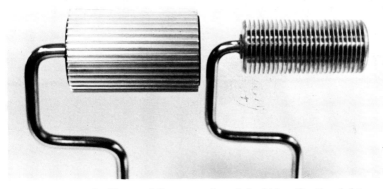

The two types of roller used for removing air bubbles. On the right is the disc roller, with the more commonly-used paddle roller on the left. Both are available in a variety of sizes.

Although it is quite easy to trim off the excess material from a mould by using a knife whilst the lamination is at the 'green' stage, there still remains the task of tidying up the edges of the moulding. Probably the single most useful tool for this job is the small angle-grinder, such as the Wolf Grinderette or its equivalent in other makes. This should be used in conjunction with a sanding disc, sitting on its rubber backing pad. Attempting to use the same type of disc and pad on an ordinary electric drill is rarely successful, for two reasons; it is often necessary to operate the grinder with one hand whilst holding the job in place with the other — and with an electric drill, this calls for an unachievable dexterity and can get down-right dangerous. Also, using an electric drill reduces the operator's field of vision, making it easy to overdo the trimming process.

Another use for the angle grinder is that it will accept a diamond-edge cutting tool, which can make light work of cutting back a thick moulding to its trim edge. The only problem here is that the discs are staggeringly expensive to purchase — about half the cost of the grinder itself! Should you be planning to do a lot of laminating, this can become cost-effective. If not, if you

An angle grinder fitted with a sanding disc. Despite its apparent age, this tool is only a couple of months old — which gives an idea of the type of accelerated wear that prevails in a glassfibre workshop.

are intending your foray into the world of glassfibre to be a one-off, then it may make more sense to use an electric jigsaw to trim through thicker mouldings.

Wherever it is necessary to cut holes into a laminated panel, it will assist matters if you have an electric drill to hand, either to make a pilot hole for the blade of an electric jigsaw or to perforate the whole outside edge of the hole, so that it can be punched out and finished. An electric drill will also prove useful for buffing the gel-coat surface of a mould or lamination, when the tool has been fitted with a lambswool polishing bonnet. When

The same grinder, five minutes later (which is why it hasn't aged any more since the previous photograph), fitted with a diamond-tipped cutting disc. This latter fitting is expensive, but worthwhile if you're planning much work in glassfibre.

using this tool, however, great care must be taken to avoid using excessive pressure, which will lead to burn marks on the surface of the lamination. Once there, such marks are all but impossible to remove.

A major problem that arises when using power tools in the laminating shop is that they do not last very long; the dust raised during the finishing process is extremely abrasive (the glass goes back to its sandy roots when reduced to dust) and this has an extremely deleterious effect on motors and bearings. The only way to enable your power tools to live out their lives to the normal span is to have them overhauled regularly. The dust normally enters the casing of a power tool through its cooling vents, but as the motor requires a constant throughflow of cooling air to maintain the correct operating temperature, never attempt to block the dust's means of entry by blanking off the cooling slots — all that will result will be a small fire inside the tool as the motor burns out.

The only other tools that are likely to be needed during the lamination process are normal DIY items such as a selection of hammers, a range of screwdrivers, a couple of chisels, a couple of clamps and a rubbing block for abrasive paper.

CHAPTER 3

PERSONAL PROTECTION

The first stop after buying tools should be to obtain a selection of basic items of protective clothing. Rubber gloves are a good item to start with, as they will not only protect your hands from the resin itself (which can become extremely uncomfortable when it attaches itself to the skin and hand hair) but also from the acetone used for cleaning tools. This is notorious for the way in which it strips the skin of its natural oils, and can lead to all manner of dermatological problems. Good old Marigold gloves, just like the ones telly mums always seem to wash up in, are about the ideal type to buy, as they are of a gauntlet design which will protect the wrists.

The choice of clothing for laminating in is entirely up to you — just do not expect to be able to wear them for anything else, as they will be ruined. I tend to wear old clothes, covered in turn by an old pair of overalls. One or two of the contract cleaning companies (Spring Grove, Initial, and so forth) offer for sale old overalls which are no longer serviceable as workwear rental items, but will be fine for use in a laminating shop. And at £2 to £3 per pair, they are extremely good value. Contact your local branch (by looking in your local classified directory under Overall Hire Services) and enquire about the availability of these items.

The rule about shoes is much the same as that for

Three items that no laminator, amateur or professional, should be without. In addition to heavyweight gloves, a pair or two of thinner washing-up type gloves should be bought. The breather mask should be used whenever trimming is being carried out. Goggles or safety glasses should be worn at all times — eyes are not replaceable.

clothes — do not expect them to be good for anything else once they have seen active service in a glassfibre workshop. And if you are working in the garage at home, take them off before entering the house; trying to remove resin and matting from a carpet is a thankless and near-impossible task. The only effective solvent for resin is acetone, and that will almost invariably strip the carpet of its colouring. Walking through to the lounge with a pair of shoes or boots that were tramping through dropped resin just a few moments earlier is a surefire way of being banned from the house henceforth, so be warned.

When you get to the finishing stage of a project, it is time to pay special attention to those most vital organs, your lungs. Wearing a mask is the basic rule, but it needs to be a proper filtered item to offer real protection against dust — an old handkerchief tied across the face Lone Ranger-style just will not do. The reasoning behind this is sensible enough; in the section on tools, I made mention of the damaging effect that glassfibre dust can have on power tools. So think what the dust can do to your lungs. And unlike power tools, you cannot just drop your breathing apparatus into the local service depot for a quick once-over.

In a similar manner, the eyes are particularly vulnerable at finishing time, and need to be properly protected

The use of a barrier cream will protect your skin from the worst ravages of the materials and solvents, and a good quality skin cleanser is the way to remove the dirt and grime that does manage to attach itself to you. Use a hand cream to restore the moisture in your skin once work has finished for the day.

by goggles. In addition to the abrasive dust, there is the ever-present threat of bits of glassfibre flying off from a panel being trimmed, so the chosen goggles must be strong enough to offer protection against this.

A couple of items from the bathroom cabinet are useful in the glassfibre business, these being talcum powder and barrier cream. Dusting the inside of rubber gloves with talc will make them a lot easier to put on, and the barrier cream will put up a reasonable fight against any drying out of the skin brought about by the acetone.

To minimize the itching, once you have finished work for the day, head straight for the shower. Start off with the water as close to cold as you can tolerate, and stay under it for a few minutes before you give yourself a scrub — this will allow the worst of the offending particles to wash off, rather than you rubbing them into your skin. The heat can be gradually turned up, once the skin is reasonably clean — had you started off with hot water, the pores of your skin would have opened up and absorbed particles of dust, which induces a rash in no time at all. All of the clothes that you have been wearing next to the skin should be washed, ideally in an automatic machine which has a bio-programme — this will give extended soaks, and help wash out the abrasive particles.

The whole business of using glassfibre materials without risk to your personal safety is covered in Chapter 14 — don't miss that bit out. As explained there, some of the chemicals are inflammable: while there is absolutely no need to have a fire if you're careful, it makes sense to be prepared in case something does go wrong, and a fire extinguisher should definitely be part of your equipment. The type recommended contains either BCF or CO_2 — water-filled ones are not suitable, as water can spread rather than extinguish burning chemicals.

PART 2

MATERIALS
AND
THEIR USE

CHAPTER 4

GEL-COAT RESIN

The gel-coat is the shiny outside surface of a moulding, a finish achieved by the use of a specific type of resin. As the name suggests, the consistency of the resin is not a million miles removed from that of an almost-set jelly, and substantially thicker than a normal lay-up resin. The principal advantage of this viscosity is that a laminator can give an even covering over a mould or former, with a uniform stress factor. And no runs, either.

Strand Glass offer one gel-coat resin, which they have rather romantically named 'Type B'. BIP offer two types, these being their general-purpose No 8181 and the fire-retardant No 8185.

Gel comes in a rather insipid and wimpish shade of pink, but should you prefer to mould in a more butch and positive colour, it is easy to tint the resin — see Chapter 6 for details. Both BIP and Strand offer a pre-tinted gel-coat resin, but this is available only in white, and costs more than standard gel resin.

Once catalysed (using the same catalyst as lay-up resin) the working time of gel is in the region of fifteen minutes, assuming the correct 2% of catalyst and a room temperature of 68°F (20°C). In cooler conditions the set-off time will be a little longer, and vice-versa. In the case of a room being far warmer than the recommended

To avoid all confusion, Strand wisely package their gel and lay-up resins quite differently. Always ensure that you purchase the catalyst for your resin — some suppliers charge extra for it, others don't.

temperature, leading to the resin going off with indecent haste, it is possible to slow the process down slightly by making a reduction in the amount of catalyst. Going down to a proportion of 1% will extend the working life of the mix. Do not go any lower than this proportion, or the gel will never harden. In counterpoint to this, never increase the amount of catalyst beyond the 3% mark in an effort to accelerate the curing process when conditions are cool.

I have seen resin mixed up in all manner of tubs, from the bottom halves of washing-up liquid bottles to plastic buckets, but the ideal receptacle for resin and catalyst has to be the little bucket-shaped tubs that are available from Strand Glass. Using one of these, pour as much gel-coat as you are likely to be able to apply within the working time of the mix, or, for a small job, as much as

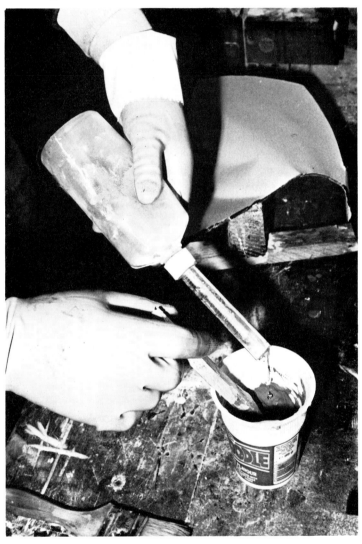

Having already added the tint to his pot of resin, Ian is seen here adding the catalyst. Stirring should be thorough, but slow. This is to avoid aeration which will cause pinholes in the finished lamination's surface.

you are likely to need.

To this can now be added the required tint pigment, using the proportions detailed in Chapter 6. Stir the two

A layer of gel is painted onto the prepared mould. The coat should be spread to a uniform thickness (thinness?) of around 0.015in (0.4mm) and left to cure before adding the backing of mat which will give the lamination strength.

The laminators employed by Cheetah Cars, of Newcastle, laying up the gel-coat onto one of their Cobra bodyshells.

thoroughly until the gel is evenly coloured. Now you can add the catalyst, taking great care not to exceed the required proportion, and also not to spill any — the catalyst used is an organic peroxide which is highly corrosive (see Chapter 14 for details of how to handle this liquid) and must be treated with the greatest degree of care and caution.

For ideal results, the industry recommends that the gel-coat should be a mere 0.015in (0.4mm) thick. Take a look at a feeler gauge to determine just how thin that is. What must be borne in mind at all times is that the gel is a surfacing, with no inherent strength — the durability of a moulding comes from the resin-impregnated matting or roving which will be the next part of the process. By applying too much gel you are inviting trouble at a later stage, as the surface will be prone to cracking.

There are other factors which must be kept to the

forefront of the mind when working with gel-coat resin. The first of these is that the gel is the part of the job which everybody will see — the outside finish. Therefore, gel must be applied evenly if a scrappy finish is to be avoided. For the same reason, avoid using a new paintbrush to apply the resin — new brushes are prone to moulting strands of bristles, and these could so easily find themselves immortalized on the outside surface of your masterpiece. It is far better to use a brush which has already seen some service laying up ordinary resin and

For small quantities of resin, a pot such as this empty (and spotlessly clean) Pot Noodle container is ideal. For larger quantities, use a larger pot.

mat, as the process will have drawn any loose bristles from their mount. Finally, the moulding will only be as good as the original from which it has been sprung. If your finished product has a rippled, lumpy or generally uneven surface, don't immediately blame the gel-coat; it could just as easily be the condition of the original that is to blame.

During its normal working time, the resin will be smooth and easy to apply, flowing nicely from the brush. As it starts to go off, it will become lumpy, and take on the consistency of porridge. Once this happens, stop working immediately, and tidy up what is already on the mould. If there is only a small amount of gel left in the pot, leave it there to harden — it can easily be bashed out later. If there is a lot of gel, pour the excess off into a suitable larger container — the heat generated by a lot of curing gel in a small area will create extremely noxious fumes — and brush out the pot to leave a smooth finish which can be removed later. Thoroughly clean out the brushes, and either start afresh if there is more gel to be applied, or go and have a cup of tea whilst you wait for the gel to dry.

CHAPTER 5

LAY-UP RESIN

There are a number of specific lay-up resins available, each with a different purpose in life. Looking first at the Strand Glass range, they offer 'Type A', which is their general purpose resin, 'Type F', which is fire-retardant, and 'Type H', which has the properties of being not only resistant to heat, but also capable of withstanding mild chemical corrosion. In contrast, the range of resins available from BIP is positively bewildering. However, as a guide I have waded through their list and come up with three equivalents to the Strand products; these are 864E for all general applications, 805 for fire-resistance, and 846 as a mild acid-resistant resin.

As with the gel-coat resin, lay-up resins are best with a catalyst mixed in a proportion of 2%, though once again this can be dropped to as low as 1% to slow down the mix set-off time. And just like gel, the catalyst proportion should never exceed 3%.

Whenever you are producing a moulding in a colour, rather than translucent resin pink, it is essential that the resin is tinted to match the gel-coat, otherwise the finished lamination will be patchy in appearance. Again, refer to Chapter 6 on pigments and tints to check out the details of colouring your resin.

Working time of lay-up resins is much the same as gel, at about fifteen minutes under ideal conditions. The way

Tinting a resin should be done by adding the pigment before the catalyst is mixed in.

to tell that a mix has gone off is that it will start to go lumpy, and string onto the brush or roller as it is removed from the mixing pot. Once this starts to happen, finish off working whatever mix is already on the job (once applied to a mould, a mix takes between twice and three times as long to go off as it would in the pot), roll out any air from the matting, and clean off the brushes, rollers and other tools before starting afresh with a new mix.

When using resin to lay up matting onto a pre-gelled surface, the first move should be to ensure that the gel surface is ready to receive the lamination. Because the air-exposed surface of a gel-coat will stay tacky for some days, it is pretty pointless waiting until the gel is smooth to the touch — instead, check that no gel transfers to your fingers when you touch the job.

Once you have the gel ready, mix up either as much resin as you need, or as much as can be applied to the mould in fifteen minutes — whichever is the smaller amount. Again, ensure that pigment tint is added and thoroughly mixed into the resin before the catalyst is added. Paint a wet coat of resin onto the gel-coat, and then apply your matting progressively, wetting it out thoroughly from the top.

When laying up, it is essential that the matting (or roving, whichever you are using) is evenly laid, smooth and flat, and completely wet — dry patches at this stage

Whilst most amateurs will only be buying small quantities of material at a time, the pro buys in bulk — hence this large bottle of catalyst, which has a measure in the tube.

As with gel-coat resin, all mixing should be thorough but slow to ensure that there is no aeration of the mix.

will harbour bubbles of air at a later stage. Because of the amount of heat that is generated by resin as it cures, take care not to apply too much at one time — consider two layers of matting, wetted thoroughly, to be the maximum. The penalty that will be paid for applying too much resin and mat in one go is that warping of the moulding will set in — and this is virtually impossible to correct.

The number of layers that a job will require is governed by several factors; the size and scale of the job, whether it is a mould from which copies will be sprung or whether it is a copy from the mould, and whether the idea of moulding in glassfibre is to save weight, by duplicating a steel panel in GRP. If the latter is the case, there is little point in replacing a steel panel with a glassfibre moulding which has so many layers that it

Once the mix is ready to use, paint over the waiting gel-coat with lay-up resin. Wearing gloves is strongly recommended to avoid skin contamination, not to mention the problems of separating cured resin and hair.

weighs more than the original!

Once you have established that the job has got as many layers as it requires (see the various projects in Part 3 for an idea of what is involved) it is time to start tidying up the job. Once the resin is completely dry, lightly sand off the inside of the moulding with coarse abrasive paper to remove any loose strands of matting. If required, the inside of the moulding can be given a finishing coat: mix up a resin and tint solution, and add a shot of liquid paraffin wax, mixing this in thoroughly before adding the normal amount of catalyst. Now carefully brush-paint this coat onto the inside of the job, being careful to avoid any runs or sags. Once dry, which will be about an hour, this will give the inside surface of the job a neat and tidy finish. The wax added will remove all traces of tackiness from the surface, rendering it smooth to the

Once the surface is covered apply the first layer of matting, press into place and wet it out using your brush as a stipple to avoid stretching the mat to the point of separation.

touch. Do not expect the finish to be shiny, for the combination of wax and resin will result in a dull sheen to the dry paint coat.

The choice of resin pot is determined by your affluence. This is a purpose-supplied item from Strand.

CHAPTER 6

PIGMENTS AND TINTS

In its natural state, resin comes in a translucent pinkish shade, though this can border on purple, depending upon the source. Likewise, gel-coat resin comes in a blancmange pink hue. Should you be intending to paint the finished moulding, then this is no problem as the wimpish appearance of the lamination will be covered by the colour coat. However, should you prefer to mould in a colour, it is possible to obtain a selection of tints which can be added to both the gel-coat and the lay-up resin.

The major supplier of tints in Britain is a Birmingham company, Llewellyn Ryland Limited, and they offer not only a hundred solid colours which comprise the British Standard range, but also a selection of further solid colours, and some very attractive metallic colourways. These vary in light-fastness, which means that some will fade slightly and others will still look as fresh as new in years to come. It appears that their cadmium-based range offers the greatest degree of resistance to fade, though at the cost of there being only a small range of colours available.

The advantage of using a pre-tinted resin and gel is that there is a guaranteed uniformity of colouration, with the moulding the same colour on both sides. A further advantage is that small scratches which would penetrate a colour paint coat will not show anything like as prominently on an impregnated panel.

Tint pigments are generally sold in small tins, with enough to treat perhaps 5 litres of resin in a container costing only £3 or so at 1986 prices. The costs vary, depending upon the range from which the colour has come — the British Standard range are the cheapest, whilst the most costly are the metallic finishes and, surprisingly, red shades.

Pigments are soluble in either acetone — the same solvent that is used for resins — or in soapy water. The tints are heavily concentrated to ensure good colouration, so they must be treated with the utmost care and caution. One tiny spot on the tip of a finger can get everywhere in no time at all, so ensure that you wash your hands and mop up any spillages before proceeding. If you end up with little daubs of yellow ochre throughout the house, you have only yourself to blame.

To use a pigment, add 10% by volume (not weight) to gel-coat resin, and stir it thoroughly before adding the catalyst, ensuring that there is an even mix. This rule of 10% applies to virtually all of the Ryland range, with the exception of black which can be added to the resin in a slightly smaller amount. It is essential that the mixing is done slowly, as too fast a stirring action can result in aeration, which will manifest itself later by air bubbles appearing on the surface of the finished job.

When pigmenting lay-up resins, a slightly smaller quantity of tint can be used, due to the thinner consistency of the resin compared to gel-coat. With either resin, it is advisable to check the colour of the finished mix against that on the colour chart from which you selected the shade, to ensure that you have the required colouration. It is also recommended that you tint enough resin to complete the project in one go, decanting the mix into smaller working pots before the catalyst is added. That way, uniformity is guaranteed. Should the mix have stood for any length of time, give it a stir before decanting to ensure that none of the pigment has

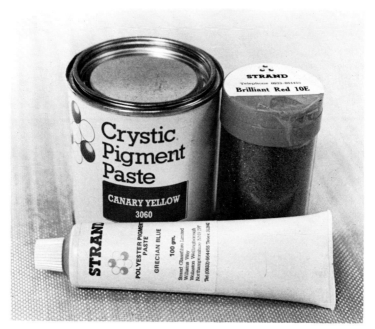

Adding pigment tints, which are available from all GRP materials suppliers, is the way of converting the basic pink resin into a shade close to that of your car. It is even possible to obtain tint pigments already impregnated with metallic particles.

settled to the bottom.

Should you find that there are problems with the colour of a finished job being patchy, this could have resulted from one of several factors; the gel-coat could have been applied unevenly, the resin used could be different (a job which has been spread over several days, and used resin from another tin to finish the lamination, for example) or the mix could have settled before the batch was used up — meaning that the last part of the job had a greater concentration of pigment than the first.

CHAPTER 7

GLASSFIBRE MATTING

The basis of most lamination processes is mat, which consists of short strands of glassfibre matted together in sheet form. These come on rolls, and in various weights, the most common being 300g per square metre (1oz per square yard), 450g (1 ½oz) and 600g (2oz). Mat is sold by the metre, in a roll width of 90 centimetres (which, for the unmetricated amongst us, is just under a yard).

The more complex a shape, the fewer layers of matting it will require, as corners, curves and ridges all add to the strength of moulding. The standard point of reference throughout this book is 450g (1 ½oz) matting, as this is by far the most common weight used throughout the industry. Therefore, wherever a project calls for matting, consider that it will be this unless otherwise stated.

Being of random construction, there is no right or wrong direction in which to lay matting, even though it does have a grain which makes it possible to tear the material in one direction only. The grain is laid lengthwise around the roll. There are a number of guidelines which need to be heeded if matting is to be used successfully.

The first of these is to ensure that the matting is thoroughly and evenly wetted out with resin, and that there is a total absence of air between the layers. Using

This is matting, available in three weights to suit different requirements. As you can see, it is made up from strands of glassfibre of random length and direction.

either a brush or roller, first paint onto the mould a thick coat of catalysed resin. Then lay the matting on, and tamp it down with the brush or roller until it achieves a uniform wetness — any mat which has dry spots will still be silvery in appearance. Once the mat is thoroughly wet, take a paddle roller (or disc roller for confined spaces) and gently but firmly run it along the wet mat. Apply enough pressure to ensure that the mat is firmly in contact with the previous layer, but not so much pressure that the strands begin to separate, leading to bald patches. Only when all traces of air have been removed can you be sure that the lamination will achieve the required strength. Where you are working into a corner that cannot be reached by a roller, use a gloved

It is essential that matting is thoroughly wetted out before rolling out any air bubbles. Keep the brush loaded with resin, and use it end-on with a stippling action to avoid damaging the matting.

finger to gently extract all traces of air.

Always work with pieces of matting that are of manageable size, in the interests of avoiding both air bubbles and getting the stuff everywhere but where it is supposed to be — on the job. Whenever a piece of matting runs off the edge of the mould, ensure that the resin saturation continues just beyond the edge, and also that the loose edge which is waving in the air is a cut one, rather than a torn one. This will ensure that the correct number of layers are evenly applied throughout the job. Finally, where pieces of matting join on a moulding, make sure that they join on torn rather than cut edges, and that they overlap slightly. This is because torn edges

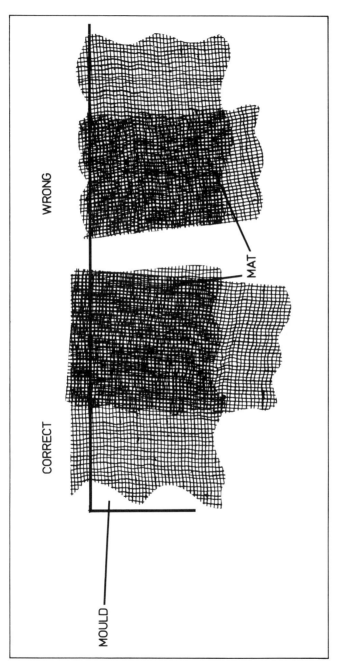

MOULD

CORRECT

WRONG

MAT

Always run the mat off the edge of the mould with a cut, rather than torn edge — this will ensure that the layers are even throughout the job, and that the eventual moulding will be sufficiently strong.

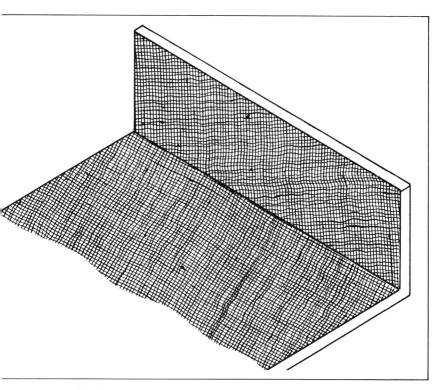

Trying to make matting take a 90° bend is an impossibility. The way to do the job is to run cut edges of the first layer of matting into the corner. Subsequent layers can be curved into the corner, as the air space will actually add strength — see Chapter 11 on strengtheners for details of the theory.

will blend in together, fooling the job into thinking that it is moulded from one big piece of matting. Cut edges will not integrate anything like as well. Apart from anything else, the finished effect of blended torn matting is far more pleasing to the eye than cut pieces are.

Where a number of amateur laminators come unstuck (literally . . .) is in trying to persuade matting to make a 90° bend. Quite simply, it will not. Because of its construction, matting must be laid on curves, and if you try to make it take a right-angle turn, it will very rapidly lift off slightly, which can mean that an air space is created. This in turn can mean that the gel-coat is

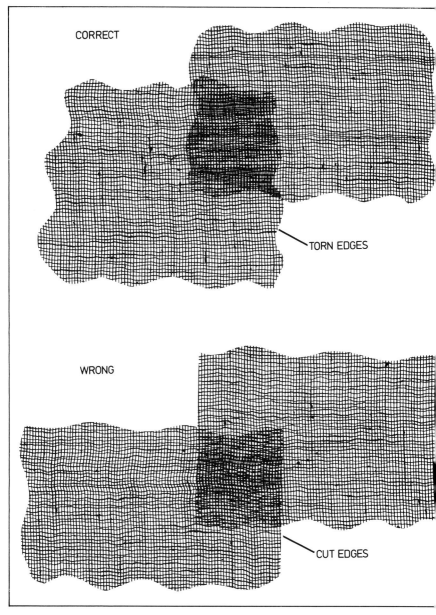

CORRECT

TORN EDGES

WRONG

CUT EDGES

Where overlapping matting, use torn, rather than cut edges. This
will ensure not only a better bonding between the two layers, but
also a tidier finish.

When working into a curve, it is often impossible to use a roller for air extraction. Instead, use your gloved finger to gently remove any bubbles.

unsupported, and will not come out of the mould with the rest of the job. Where a moulding calls for an internal 90° bend, lay pieces of matting so that cut edges are abutted into the corner. Once a single layer of matting has been affixed to the gel-coat and allowed to dry, subsequent layers can be allowed to form their own little curves — any air spaces which result at this stage can actually strengthen a job by acting as box-sections. See Chapter 11 on strengtheners for a further explanation of this concept.

On an external 90° bend, this will not work, as there will be no direct wrapping of the bend. What to do here is to use a strip of tissue (see Chapter 9) over the edge of the bend, and hold this in place with matting cut to the edges as previously. Subsequent layers can then be wrapped over to avoid any localized weakness in the moulding.

The last thing to remember about chopped strand mat is that it will only work effectively if clean. Any pieces which have been contaminated by a previous mix of resin, and then allowed to dry out, should have the offending area removed if a large piece of mat, or be thrown away if a small piece. Applying a piece of contaminated matting to a job will result in the offending piece merely being glued into place, rather than integrating with the other matting around it — which is hardly an ideal way to gain strength within a moulding. Matting which has been allowed to get very dusty can similarly resist wetting by the resin, and weaken the result.

CHAPTER 8

GLASSFIBRE ROVING

Woven roving is designed as an alternative to chopped strand glassfibre matting, but differs substantially from that material in that instead of being of random short strand construction, it is formed of continuous filaments of glassfibre woven into a uniform cloth-like pattern.

As with matting, roving is available in a selection of weights to suit different applications. These are 280g per square metre (about 1oz per square yard), 560g (2oz approximately) and 830g (equivalent to about 3oz per square yard), and again are sold by the metre from a roll 90 centimetres wide.

The major advantage that roving offers over matting is that its texture makes it far more flexible, which can be quite a boon on certain jobs. It also offers a slight weight saving over mat, though this is countered to some degree by the additional amount of resin needed to wet out the roving compared to a similar area laid up with matting. The disadvantage of roving is that it is more expensive than matting, with a premium of something like 30% to pay over the cost of the equivalent chopped strand mat. Because of the plainweave format, it is recommended that each layer of roving is laid at an angle of 45° to the previous layer.

Despite the fact that it will hold substantially more resin than matting does, roving is less susceptible to

Woven rovings, formed textile-fashion from continuous glassfibre filaments, are available in three weights; the two shown here are 830g and 280g. These are laid up in the same way as matting, and offer a great degree of strength when cured.

excesses of trapped air, but all the same does need to be rolled down with a paddle roller to extract any bubbles. Unlike matting, it is impossible to tear the edge of roving: instead, it must be cut, preferably with a pair of substantial scissors — tailors' shears are the ideal (but not if you or someone else will want to use them for tailoring again, as the glass fibres will blunt them fairly rapidly). Failing this, use a Stanley knife and straight-edge to make the cuts.

When joining pieces of roving during the lamination process, overlap the edges by an inch or so, to ensure full coverage and strength. Being woven, roving has a warp and a weft, and just like any other fabric, cut across one and the other will fray — which can be a pain, as the loose strands can get caught up in the brush or wrapped around the roller applying the resin, and this in turn can lead to the whole of the piece pulling out of shape and place. With either means of resin application, work from the centre of the piece of roving towards the outside edges to minimize this problem.

As with matting, it is impossible to get roving to form a sharp angle, as it too prefers to be moulded in a gentle curve. Again, the key to success with an unavoidable

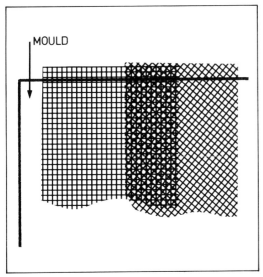

Because it is imposs-ible to tear roving, it must be cut. The second layer should be cut at 45° to the first to increase the lamina-tion strength. Note also that it must be over-lapped beyond the edge of the mould, to ensure adequate coverage of the lamination.

As with matting, it is necessary to lay cut edges of roving into a corner, rather than try to make the first layer adopt a sharp 90° bend. Subsequent layers can be run through the cor-ner, to form a small hollow section.

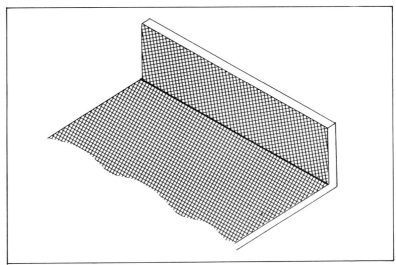

angle is to butt together sharp cut edges. When working with roving on this problem, lay the material down evenly to ensure that the abutting edges stay together — working from the centre of the piece can, in this instance, backfire by either pulling the edges apart to leave a gap or pushing them too close together so that they buckle.

CHAPTER 9

GLASSFIBRE TISSUE

This is another of those products with a self-explanatory name, as it has the appearance of domestic Kleenex-type tissue. It is made from fine-strand glassfibre, and has two distinct and very different uses. The first of these is facing the matting side of a lamination, smoothing over what would otherwise be a relatively coarse surface. However, as a similar finish can often be achieved by flatting off the surface with abrasive paper and then applying a paint coat (a process detailed in Chapter 5) this can be something of an unnecessary expense.

The other application for tissue is as an alternative to gel-coat. Should you prefer your moulding to have a softly-grained surface in place of the hard glaze resulting from the use of gel-coat resin, then this is the way to achieve it. Interior trim such as the facia and door panels is the sort of application that this type of finish suits particularly, although it can also be useful when a mould or buck is less than perfect — the less-harsh finish of a tissue surfacing can hide a multitude of sins that would be highlighted by the shiny finish of a gel-coat.

Surfacing tissue is available in only one weight, which avoids neatly any problem of deciding the right one for the job, and is sold by the linear metre off the roll (which conforms to the usual width of 90cm) in the same way as matting and roving. Unlike the other two forms of

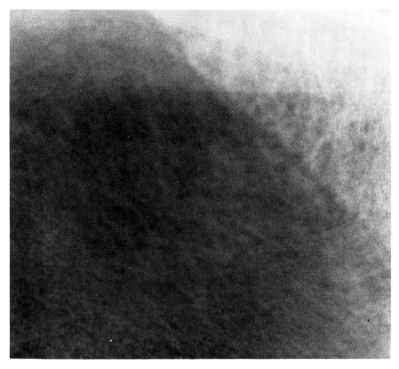

Surfacing tissue is a particularly fine-grained glassfibre material, designed for draping over complex curves and giving a smooth finish to laminations.

glassfibre textile, tissue has a right and wrong side, the former being smooth and slightly glazed, whilst the latter has a mass of little hairs protruding from its matt surface. Lay the tissue smooth side down.

To use tissue in lieu of gel-coat resin, start by wetting out the surface of the mould with regular lay-up resin, and then gently lay the tissue with its smooth side towards the mould. Unlike gel, any joins in a tissue surface will show, so it is essential that you either use one piece to cover the entire mould, or position any joins in such a place that they will be hidden from view on the completed moulding.

The main precaution to take when working with tissue is to remember that it is infinitely more fragile than matting, and so needs to be treated with tender loving care throughout the lay-up process. It will stretch slightly, which makes it useful for dealing with a curved surface, but care must be taken if it is not to split when being tamped down. Unlike gel-coat resin, there is no reason to wait around for the resin to dry off before adding a layer of matting — in fact, it makes sense in view of the fragility of tissue to back it up with a layer of mat before rolling the lamination down to release any air bubbles. When using tissue and having the intention of backing it up with a woven roving in order to add strength to a lamination, first use a single layer of matting on top of the tissue as there is a tendency for the texture of the roving to show through the tissue.

To use tissue as a means of backing up the rough side of a moulding in order to make it more presentable, first sand down the moulding to remove any wayward

One of the applications for tissue is in moulding grained surfaces, such as the door panel trims of this experimental GM car, the Equus.

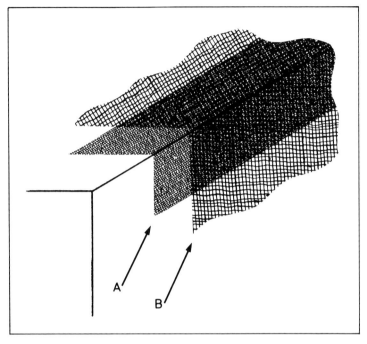

Another use for tissue is in surfacing outside 90° bends, where the tissue (A) is laid over the gel, and then backed up by regular matting (B).

strands of glassfibre — otherwise, they will penetrate the tissue and rather defeat the object of the exercise. The problem of joins in tissue is less critical on the reverse side of a job, but all the same try to minimize or conceal any joints. Should it be necessary to roll the tissue surface in order to remove air bubbles, do so with the lightest of touches, otherwise the surface could stretch or separate — which would again defeat the object of the exercise. The ideal way to back up a moulding with a tissue layer is to apply the latter before the matting has dried — that way, everything integrates neatly, and a lot of work is avoided.

CHAPTER 10

MAKING FORMERS

Unless you are moulding from an existing panel (duplicating a steel car wing, for example, in an effort to save weight) it will be necessary to produce some type of former from which to produce a mould, which will in turn be used to make the duplicate.

For forming simple shapes with no compound curves, the most useful material in which to invest is hardboard, with a timber frame for added strength if necessary. However, should you need or wish to produce a shape with a little more complexity, such as an air scoop or a belly pan, a more versatile material will be needed.

Polyurethane foam is quite useful stuff, and is available in a variety of sheet sizes and thicknesses. It can be bonded both to itself and to other materials with glue or lay-up resin, and can be shaped using a Surform plane, sandpaper, or a file. Foam is also available in a two-part, mix-it-yourself kit from Strand Glass, and this can be useful should you have an existing basic shape which you would like to integrate or incorporate into your new moulding. Always wear a face mask when working with polyurethane foam, as the dust produced by sanding or filing it will irritate the lungs and, in the case of the two-part system, the gases given off during the process are highly poisonous. Using polyurethane foam brings with it one immediate disadvantage, in that it cannot be

Polyurethane foam, as well as being available in sheet form in a variety of thicknesses, can be had in a two-part pack, from Strand.

separated from any resin with which it comes into contact. This means that using it as a former from which to spring a mould calls for the foam buck to be made slightly undersize, then clad in resin and matting or roving, before finishing with filler to a suitably smooth finish. Only when the surface is as you want the finished product to be can you make a mould from which to produce a lightweight, all-glassfibre duplicate.

Where foam really scores is in adding inner strength to a hollow moulding, or for making buoyancy tanks in boats and surfboards; make up the moulding, pour in the foam mixture (which should be done immediately after

When the two parts are mixed together, you have a few seconds . . .

. . . before the foam expands to many times its original size. Wear a mask when mixing — the fumes given off are cyanide-related, and highly toxic.

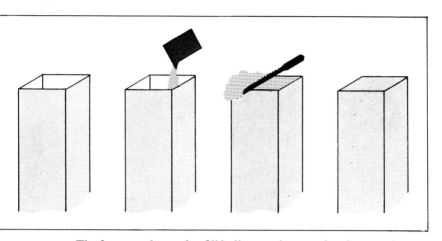

The foam can be used to fill hollow sections, such as bumper bars or sills — though originally intended as a means of adding buoyancy to boats, foam also offers a good deal of additional strength and can be usefully employed on many cars. Prepare the item to be filled, mix and pour the foam, trim off the excess once hardened, and laminate on an end cap.

combining the two components of the foam pack, as working time allowed is minimal) and leave the foam to set. Once hard, the open face into which the mix has been poured can be trimmed off with a file or Surform and sealed with glassfibre.

As the foam is semi-rigid, the surface of a moulding thus filled is given a great deal of support from within, and there is consequently little chance of minor dents doing any lasting damage. What is more, being air-filled, the moulding will float indefinitely. Whilst there is little call for buoyancy tanks on cars, the concept of foam-filled bumper bars or sill sections is an attractive one.

Perforated zinc sheeting, intended for use on body panel repairs as a means of support for glassfibre patches or for body filler, is also a useful material for moulding shapes. I have seen this used to great effect over contoured pieces of wood sheet and it could just as easily be draped over bent wire formers (welding rod is ideal for this) or small-bore pipe, such as brake line Bundy piping. The zinc sheet is very flexible and can easily be made to follow most contours. Once skimmed with body filler and sanded to shape, this can be the ideal way of creating a complex shape from which to mould.

When it comes to body filler, buying large amounts can become an expensive proposition, even when 5kg tins are purchased. A far cheaper alternative is to make up your own filler mix, using filler powder (which is only talcum, or French chalk) and mixing it into lay-up resin. A basic mix of two parts chalk to one part resin is about right, though this can be adjusted either way to suit your specific requirements. To ensure an even consistency, blend in the chalk a little at a time, stirring slowly to avoid aeration. Once the basic mix is achieved, it can be stored for some time in an airtight tin and catalysed (with standard resin catalyst) as required in the amounts

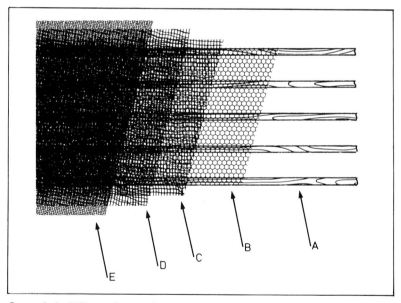

Scratch-building a former is time-consuming, but can be the only way of achieving originals for some shapes. Start with a wood frame (A) onto which is draped perforated zinc sheet (B). Two layers of matting (C & D) can then be laminated into place with catalysed lay-up resin, and finished off with a single layer of tissue (E). The surface can then be readied for moulding from by building up with filler and sanding back to a good, smooth finish.

For odd little bits of detail on a basic shape, childrens' Plasticine can be extremely useful, because of its easily-worked pliability.

needed. The proportion of catalyst should be the same 2% as used in the resin in its original state.

In addition to standard filler powder, it is also possible to obtain a number of others for specific applications. For instance, Strand Glass offer their BLR 2, which is an ultra-fine dust for use on fine castings, and Q-Cel, which is a lightweight cellular compound, but these are of little interest to anybody engaged in automotive applications for glassfibre. You might as well stick to the basic filler powder, and save some money.

Another available product which can be of use in producing former bucks is loose chopped strand glassfibre, which is mixed in with resin to produce a high-bulk filler with properties somewhere between body filler and a finished laminate. Whilst it will make up to a greater bulk than filler, it has the disadvantage of being far more difficult to finish to a final shape because of its greater hardness. For this reason, its usefulness is debatable — I feel that using filler over a mesh or wooden former is of greater use to the laminator making automotive panels.

CHAPTER 11

REINFORCEMENT

On certain panels, it is necessary to add extra strength by incorporating some form of stiffening or strengthening. Car bonnets are an ideal illustration of this, as their area is generally so great that the centre of the panel would sag if the moulding was of uniform thickness throughout. Some form of central support is definitely required if the desired finished appearance of the panel is to be achieved.

The single most useful product for performing this task is paper rope. This is available in a variety of thicknesses, and has absolutely no intrinsic strength. It will, however, make a subsequent layer of matting or roving adopt a channel shape, which is very strong indeed.

The rope should be affixed to the moulding by either resin or filler, and then laminated over with at least one layer, but preferably two or three, of matting or roving. To ensure that the panel will follow the required shape it is necessary to add the strengthening whilst the basic moulding is still in its mould — otherwise, the relatively flimsy panel could flex before the strengthening is added, and the latter will then ensure that it stays twisted throughout the rest of its days.

I have from time to time come across panels which show from the outside exactly where the stiffening ribs

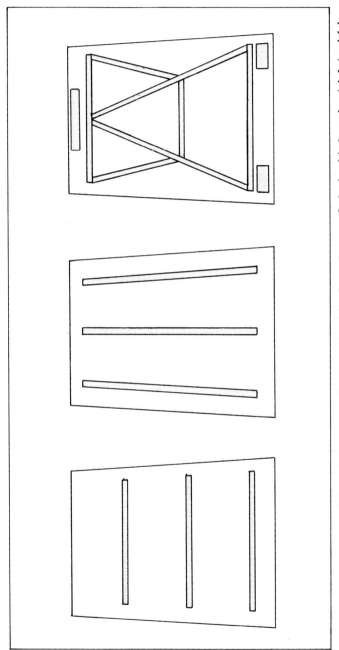

Three approaches to providing reinforcement for the underside of a car bonnet. Only the third version (right), with its triangulation, will be really effective; the other two will each offer resistance to bending in one direction only.

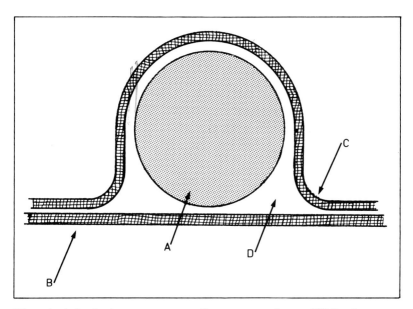

The principle of using paper rope to form a strengthener. Whilst the rope itself (A) is weak and flimsy, when it is laid on a panel (B) and laminated over (C) it forms a hollow channel section (D) in the cured glassfibre.

have been added on the underside. This is because the ribs have been added before the basic moulding has cured properly, and the extra weight of the lamination around the stiffeners or the shrinkage as it cured has made an impression on the gel-coat. The way to avoid this is to leave the basic panel in the mould to cure properly before adding the strengthening.

The arrangement of strengthening ribs is important if they are to fulfill their function correctly. For instance, there is little point in adding ribs to a car bonnet if they are all arranged in one direction only; the panel will still want to twist in all directions. By far the greatest torsional stiffness will be achieved by arranging the strengtheners in a triangular or cruciform shape.

Should you wish to combine a stiffener with some form of sound-deadener or a panel to absorb body boom, then it would be advisable to use polyurethane foam sheet of perhaps 25mm thickness bonded to the panel, and then laminated over. For the best grip and strength, cut out a couple of suitable shapes from the centre of the panel. This will then allow the subsequent layer of matting to meet with the original panel not only at the outside edges of the foam stiffener, but also at a number of points within the panel. Bearing in mind what was said in Chapter 7 on matting and its inability to form neat 90° bends, bevel the various edges of the foam insert before affixing it to the panel. Noise-deadening panels such as these are useful on bonnets, whilst anti-boom properties can be exploited on the roof panel, or perhaps the door skins. To avoid any possible confusion, note that we are talking about *polyurethane* foam, used for a whole variety of insulation purposes in industry: expanded *polystyrene,* the white, crumbly stuff used for packing and ceiling tiles, is unfortunately not applicable here as it dissolves in resin to make a gooey mess.

Another suitable stiffening material is wood, in either batten or sheet form. This has a little more strength than

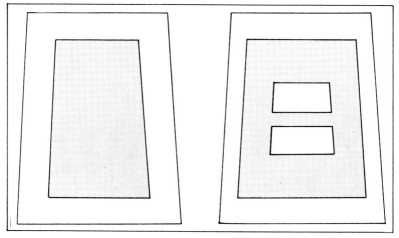

Instead of paper rope it is possible to use polyurethane foam sheet which will provide soundproofing as well as reinforcement. A single piece of foam (left) will work alright, but a couple of central cutouts (right) will enable the reinforcing lamination to be bonded to the original panel more securely and so add to the overall rigidity.

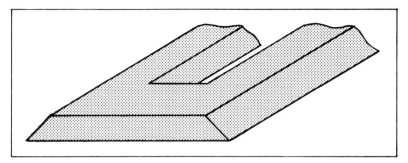

Bevel the edges of the foam to allow the matting reinforcement to curve easily over onto the panel.

the foam referred to earlier, but once again the prime stiffening will come from the shape that a subsequent layer of matting will be forced to adopt. The biggest single disadvantage that wood has is its weight,

Moulding in an air scoop like this Pro-Stock style addition to Ian Franz's Mopar-powered Marina drag racer serves the secondary purpose of strengthening the bonnet panel. Complex shapes in glassfibre are always more rigid than featureless, flat panels (assuming comparable thickness of lamination), a principle well worth remembering at the design stage.

especially when compared to the relative feather-lightness of polyurethane foam. Where wood is at its most useful is on bonnets, boots and doors, to form a durable and strong base on which to mount hinges and lock assemblies. As with the foam, it is essential to bevel the edges of the timber before laminating over it. To affix the wood itself to the panel prior to adding another layer or two of matting or roving, use body filler.

Going back briefly to car bonnets, it is worth remembering that the addition of a hood scoop will add a vast amount of strength to an otherwise flimsy panel, simply because its own shape acts as a stiffener.

What must be borne in mind at all times is that you are aiming to add stiffness and rigidity to a panel, and that such additions will come primarily from the skin laid over whatever material you choose as a former, and not from the former itself. This means that whilst a piece of 25mm × 6mm steel strap will have a great deal of intrinsic strength, once it has been bonded to a panel and laminated over it will add no more strength than would a piece of erstwhile floppy paper rope — and the steel weighs a darned sight more.

CHAPTER 12

RELEASE AGENTS

When one resin is laid directly onto another, which is what happens every time a gel-coat is applied to a mould as the first part of the copying process, the adhesive qualities of the resin would ensure a solid, even bond, glueing the mould and copy together with a staggering degree of success. The idea, however, is to produce a copy from the mould, and then to separate the two so that the copy can be used. Consequently, some form of release agent is required which will allow the gel-coat to flow smoothly over the mould at the laying-up stage, yet prevent it from sticking when the time is right to spring the copy from the mould. There are a number of different products which will allow this to happen, the most common being wax. However, not just any wax will do; many wax polishes contain silicone, and for our purpose it is essential that the wax is entirely free of silicone. To be safe, stick to the products of a team of busy worker bees. A silicone wax will lead to an oil-on-water effect when the resin is applied to the moulding; it will appear to paint on properly, but ten minutes later, you will find that the resin has separated into little pools.

There are various beeswaxes available, in a variety of different sizes of tin from 500g through to 4kg. Strand Glass also offer a wax in liquid form, which is available in either a US pint or US gallon — each of which is slightly

Applying a coat of PVA to a mould which has been thoroughly waxed. Unlike when laying up resin, the brush applying PVA should be kept only lightly loaded and the thinnest of coats applied.

smaller than the equivalent Imperial measure.

A single coat of wax is inadequate as an effective release agent; a fresh mould should be given at least four, and as many as six, separate coats. These should be applied in accordance with the instructions on the tin, and then buffed off to a deep shine before applying the next coat.

On a mould with a gel-coat facing, the wax can be applied directly to the surface. However, should you be moulding from a fabricated former which has a slightly porous surface (such as one which has been finished with body filler) it will be necessary to seal the mould first.

A selection of the waxes available from Strand Glassfibre. The bottle at the back contains PVA — the cans are labelled with their contents. Only use a silicone-free wax for mould release applications.

This is easiest done by using a proprietary sealer, such as Strand's Release Agent No 1. This is a compound in liquid form, and is to be brushed on. More than one coat may be required, depending on the porosity of the mould surface. Once the first coat has dried, inspect the surface thoroughly to see if a further coat is required. In addition to filler, this sealant can also be used on leathercloth or wood. Applying several light coats is preferable to one heavy one, in the interests of a good, even finish.

Should the surface of the mould be slightly uneven, bearing in mind that any imperfections will be highlighted by the gel-coat of the subsequent copy, it is worthwhile spending a little time and a lot of elbow grease on compounding the surface before applying any wax. Any good compound (available from car accessory shops as well as from glassfibre suppliers) will suffice for

For cleaning up the surface of a slightly uneven mould, use a good-quality compound to remove the high spots then apply wax as detailed in the text.

this task. Ensure that all traces of the compound are removed from the mould before going near it with the wax.

Once the layers of wax have been applied, it is time to use the next product for aiding release, PVA. This is a liquid solution of PolyVinyl Alcohol, and should be applied sparingly — too heavy a coat will result in sags and runs. For the easiest application, use a sponge, unless you are certain that you can be capable of the lightest of touches with a paintbrush. Should you choose the latter method, take pains to ensure that there are no stray brush hairs on the mould, as these will transfer themselves into the gel-coat of the subsequent copy to be sprung from the mould.

Once the copy has been made and then sprung from the mould, wash off all traces of the PVA (which dries a light blue/purple shade) with warm soapy water, and examine the mould and copy to ensure that all is as it should be, with no damage to either. The mould can then be stored away until it is needed again, and the copy trimmed and finished. When the time comes to use the mould again, repeat the process from the waxing stage onwards to ensure an easy release for the new copy moulding.

When the surface to be compounded is large, it may be worthwhile investing in a polishing head for your drill or grinder — take care not to apply too much pressure, though; this would irreparably damage the mould surface by cutting grooves into the gel coat.

CHAPTER 13

OTHER PRODUCTS

Whilst the previous nine chapters have covered most of the items which are of use in the various applications and projects mentioned throughout the book, there are a number of other glassfibre products which you may come across during your forays into suppliers, and it is worth taking a little space to explain what these are and the applications for which they are intended. I have listed them in alphabetical order, in the interests of simplicity.

Accelerator. In order to time the curing period of resins, it is necessary to add an accelerator, in specific and carefully measured amounts. Most resins are supplied with the accelerator already mixed in, primarily because of the volatile nature of the substance. However, it is possible to obtain resin which has not been pre-accelerated, and for this reason it is also possible to obtain the agent separately. Accelerator is a solution of cobalt in styrene, and should only be added into 'virgin' resin, to a proportion of not more than 2% by weight — never add extra accelerator into pre-accelerated resin. Also, never allow accelerator to come into direct contact with standard MEKP catalyst — an uncontrollable explosion is the inevitable outcome. Should you have both products in your workshop, keep them totally separate from each other. Unless you have a pressing reason to do otherwise, stick to pre-accelerated resin and avoid the complications of this substance.

Casting resin. This is a glass-clear resin specifically available for those on this earth who like to make paperweights in their spare time, of the sort that have a flower, dead fly or whatever immortalized in the middle. I can find no sensible application for this material in the

Glassfibre tape is designed for fast repair jobs, joins between two pieces of laminate, or reinforcing edges of mouldings. Different widths are available.

automotive field — unless you would like to have a paperweight which envelopes that twisted con-rod from your previous engine. . . .

Filletting wax. This is a soft wax available in thin strips, which is applied to the inside of shapes to radius a bend. For automotive applications, it is probably more advisable to use body filler for this purpose, because of its greater durability.

Furane resin. This is a high-gloss two-pack resin (using a special catalyst, as MEKP catalyst will not work, and should not be tried) which gives a good coating quality on absorbent surfaces. However, I have yet to come across a necessary car application for this — gel-coat and lay-up resins are capable, between them, of dealing with just about any automotive contingency.

Glassfibre tape. This is designed for fast repairs and for joining together separate pieces of glassfibre laminate. Available in a variety of widths from 25mm (1in) to 152mm (6in) and sold by the metre from a 50 metre roll, it is a woven tape of herringbone construction with a selvedged edge. It is difficult to obtain in weights other than its standard 450g per square metre, and is relatively expensive. Whilst it is undoubtedly good for its intended purposes, and can also be useful as a tidy edging strip, it can do very little more than strips of matting or roving could — and they work out to be a lot less expensive.

Metal powders. By mixing in an equal proportion of metal powder to lay-up resin, it is possible to get a realistic metal effect on a finished lamination. Available in aluminium, bronze, copper or brass, this is quite expensive (at 1986 prices, up to £35 per 5kg) and an equally effective finish could be achieved by using a good grade of metallic paint over a standard lamination. Of interest with this product is the way in which it is recommended that the powder is added after the catalyst, to ensure even dispersion — which means that working times are reduced and could render it pretty impractical for a sizeable or complicated moulding.

Resin stripping solution. This is a caustic-based solution which is specifically intended for cleaning set resin from tools and brushes by leaving them to soak in it overnight. Being both poisonous (it gives off caustic fumes which are extremely toxic) and corrosive, the greatest care must be taken when using it. On no account should it be allowed to come into contact with the skin or eyes. There is also a tendency for pressure to build within the can, so great caution must be exercised when opening the container.

Scrim. This is a useful product which falls somewhere between matting and woven roving, being a lightweight woven glassfibre fabric. Because of its construction it has excellent draping characteristics, and also gives a neat and tidy finish. Use as matting or roving, and take great care not to stretch or distort it. It is available in a selection of weights from 127g ($\frac{1}{3}$oz) to 300g (1oz) and in either open weave or satin weave finish. As with other matting products, it is sold by the metre in a width of 90cm, and cost-wise works out roughly the same as the equivalent woven roving.

Spun roving. This is a spun string of glassfibre filament, intended primarily for use in equipment which sprays chopped glassfibre and catalysed resin to form a lamination. It has another use, this being to wind it around cylindrical mouldings, where a continuous filament can add a great deal of strength. However, I have yet to find a sufficient excuse for using this material in hand-laid DIY automotive applications.

Styrene. This is a solvent for resin, and is used to thin resin down for spraying for primer coats on particularly porous materials such as wood. Mix this in with the resin before adding the catalyst, in a proportion of not more than one part styrene to twenty parts resin for surface coating, or three parts styrene to a hundred parts resin for spraying. In either case, the proportion should be by volume, and not by weight. Once again, there is very little application for this product in hand lay-up.

CHAPTER 14

MATERIALS AND SAFETY

Do not, whatever you do, skip over this chapter. Throughout the book, I have mentioned the dangers of both the materials and processes involved in the production of glassfibre laminations. I have attempted in this chapter to explain ways of overcoming the various problems, should they arise. Again, in the interests of simplicity, I have listed the various hazards in alphabetical order. Do take time to digest what I have to say in this chapter; should you have an accident and then decide to look up in here what you are supposed to do, it may well be too late by the time you have found the relevant section. So read and memorize the following details before you go near the workshop; it may save a lot of agony later.

Accelerator. Being a cobalt-styrene blend, this material has two hazards; it is poisonous, and it is capable of a chemical interaction with catalyst MEKP causing an explosion. If any comes into contact with the eyes, wash out immediately with lots of clean water. Avoid breathing the fumes by wearing a face mask: if fumes are accidentally inhaled, go outside and gulp in as much clean air as possible until you feel normal again. In the event of skin contact, wash off immediately under running water. Get a medical check-up immediately after eye or breathing contact. Do not keep in proximity to catalyst MEKP.

Acetone is virulent stuff, having a remarkable capability to strip the skin of its natural oils — which leads rapidly to a nasty form of dermatitis. The first rule, therefore, is to avoid all possible direct contact with this chemical. A barrier cream should be used before starting work, and replenished regularly throughout the day — every time you have washed your hands, apply another blob of barrier cream. Once work has finished for the day, use a good-quality hand cream, such as Vaseline's Intensive Care — this will help your skin to recover before any damage is done. Never, ever, allow acetone to come into contact with any other part of the body. Should you be unfortunate enough to get a splash of this chemical in your eye, wash it out at once with copious quantities of cold water, and seek immediate medical attention. Although it is highly unlikely, should some freak accident result in your swallowing acetone, induce vomiting by drinking a strong salt water solution, then drink as much water as possible. Again, seek immediate medical attention.

Acetone is not only dangerous to the skin and eyes and extremely toxic, but is also highly inflammable. Should there be a fire — which is a situation that should never be allowed to happen if safety procedures are adhered to, such as allowing no naked flames anywhere near exposed acetone, and not smoking in the workshop at any time — use either a BCF, carbon dioxide (CO_2), or dry powder extinguisher. Do not use water, as this will not extinguish the flames, but merely spread the acetone, which will still be alight. When burning, this chemical gives off highly toxic fumes. Should these be inhaled, gulp in as much clear air as possible, and get immediate medical help.

As with all other chemicals, acetone should be stored in nothing other than a proper metal container (it will melt plastic before your very eyes) clearly marked, and well out of the reach of children.

Catalyst. The catalyst that is used for most resin applications is methyl ethyl ketone peroxide (MEKP), and is particularly dangerous. Therefore, it should only be handled with the utmost caution and care. Firstly, only ever use the supplied measure to dispense the liquid. Secondly, do not allow it to come anywhere near undiluted accelerator — as explained in relation to that substance, when the two meet, an explosion follows rapidly. Thirdly, do not allow the catalyst to come into contact with any part of your body. If it splashes your skin, wash it off immediately with running water. If swallowed, induce vomiting by taking a salt-water emetic, and get immediate medical assistance. Should any catalyst splash into your eye, wash it out immediately with a cold water eyewash, and seek medical help immediately. To be quite safe, I would recommend that you wear goggles whenever handling this potentially nasty stuff.

Whilst catalyst has a quite high flashpoint (80°C), do not let this lull you into a false sense of security — given the opportunity, it will burst into fierce flames, emitting particularly poisonous fumes as it does so. Therefore, do not allow the liquid to be used anywhere near a naked flame, cigarette, or similar. Water will douse the flames of a *small* amount of blazing catalyst, but to be on the safe side, use a BCF or CO_2 extinguisher. Finally, in the event of a spillage of catalyst, do not attempt to mop up the liquid, but wash it away with copious quantities of water.

Glassfibre matting, roving and tissue. Provided that all the care and attention recommendations detailed in Chapter 3 are followed, there is little danger attached to the use of these materials. Glassfibre is famous for its fire-resistance, so there is little danger of scrap material bursting into flames.

Pigment. Being polyester-based, pigment tints are toxic, and should be treated carefully. As they are water-soluble, the correct way to deal with any accidental contact is to wash the affected area immediately. Use an eye-bath and copious clear water to treat splashes into the eye, and take a salt-water emetic followed by large amounts of fresh water to deal with accidental swallowing of pigments. For skin contact, wash the affected area with soap and water until clear of all traces. Should there be any lingering discomfort following the treatment of eye or oral contact, seek medical attention.

The flashpoint of pigment is high, at 65°C, but it is nonetheless a combustible substance. Therefore, keep it away from naked lights, etc, and store away from direct heat. Spillages are best treated by first absorbing the excess in sand or soak-up granules, and then washing away the remainder with soapy water.

Polyurethane foam. This is evil stuff if mishandled. Firstly, when mixing a two-pack foam for injection, isocyanate fumes are emitted — they are of the same family as cyanide, and equally poisonous. The first sign of being affected by these fumes is irritation of the nostrils and throat. Should you feel this, remove yourself immediately into the fresh air, and stay there until all feels normal again. Were you to stay in contact with the fumes, drowsiness would follow quite soon, followed rapidly by a lapse into unconsciousness — from which death could result. Don't say I haven't warned you.

Direct physical contact with foam is to be avoided at all costs, as the foam will attach itself to the skin with staggering efficiency. Any accidental contact should be treated by removing all traces of foam before it has time to set — once hard, it will be an extremely difficult material to remove from the skin. Strand Glass supply a skin cleanser called Kerocleanse which will assist in removing the still-liquid foam from the skin, so keep a container of this handy.

Goggles *must* be worn when using foam mix, as it is virtually impossible to remove any of the stuff from the eyes.

There are no special flammability problems with

foam, but should any ignite as a result of perhaps an acetone fire, use a BCF extinguisher to deal with it.

PVA release agent. PVA is alcohol-based, and so it follows that the main hazard with the liquid is its flammability — a flashpoint of minus 20°C should say it all. Treat the agent as you would petrol — no naked flames, and so forth — and you will not go far wrong. As with any inflammable liquid, use a BCF extinguisher, or one which employs CO_2. Do not use water under any circumstances, as this will only spread the fire. Use absorbent granules to soak up any spillages, and remove them to a safe place when they have done their job.

Although to a lesser degree, PVA will act on your skin in the same way as acetone, stripping away the natural oils. Therefore, always use a barrier cream, and wear gloves when dealing with release agents. Accidental eye contact should be treated by using an eye-bath with lots of fresh water. If swallowed, encourage the PVA to go back to where it came from by using an emetic followed by lots of fresh water.

Resins. Due to the heat generated during the curing process, the principal risk with resins is that of fire — particularly from quantities of catalysed resins which have started to go off in the pot. Remove material in this state to a safe place where it cannot ignite other waste materials — and the greater the area over which it is dispersed, the safer the disposal process. Should you have a fire, deal with it by either dry powder or BCF extinguisher — water is again not recommended.

Accidental spillage is best dealt with by absorbing the resin in soak granules or dry sand, and then removing the waste to a safe place.

During the curing process, resin gives off toxic fumes which should be avoided — the symptoms are similar to those of foam mix, with irritation of the breathing equipment followed by drowsiness, and subsequently a lapse into unconsciousness. I far prefer to get into that state by the liberal application of Bell's or Remy Martin

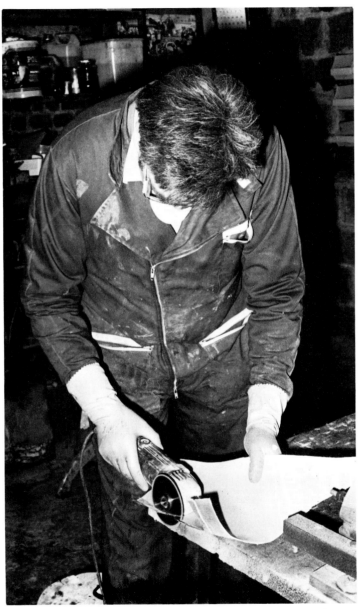

The right way to do it: whilst finishing off a lamination using an angle grinder, Ian is modelling a face mask, safety glasses and gloves, as well as overalls — thus ensuring that nothing can get to his skin, eyes or lungs.

— it isn't as immediately fatal!

Should you have any accidental contact with resin mix, use an eye-bath and lots of fresh water to deal with a splash in that area, and an emetic and lots of water to cope with an accidental swallowing. Resin is best removed from the skin with Kerocleanse, followed by soap and water.

PART 3

PRACTICAL PROJECTS

CHAPTER 15

GLASSFIBRE SHEET

Jolly useful stuff, flat glassfibre sheet. For instance, it makes a superb forming material, especially when used in conjunction with polyurethane foam. Then there is its unrivalled usefulness when producing one-off mouldings such as air intakes and liner panels.

Producing flat sheet is simplicity itself, and the process makes excellent practice in the art of lamination, ready for the more complicated mouldings which follow. The ideal former from which to make the sheet is laminated chipboard, such as that sold under the Contiplas trade mark. When I started out, I wondered why glass sheet wouldn't work. After all, it is smooth, and very flat. I soon discovered that it is *too* smooth and flat — and that it was virtually impossible to separate the glassfibre from the glass.

The chipboard should be prepared by giving it several applications of release wax, each one being buffed off before the next is applied. Final preparation is a matter of a thinly-brushed coat of PVA, which should be left for five minutes or so to dry off.

The amount of gel that is mixed depends entirely on the area that you intend to cover. As a guide, one square metre of surface requires 450 grammes of mixed gel-coat resin. If you intend to tint the gel, this should be done whilst waiting for the PVA to dry. Take great care to

ensure that the pigment is added in the correct proportion, and mixed thoroughly. Only when the pigment is
evenly dispersed should you add the catalyst, which
should again be completely mixed into the gel.

Using a brush, paint on a thin coat of gel over the area
that you intend to cover, aiming for the thickness of
0.015in (0.4mm) that we talked about in Chapter 4.
Leave this to set to the point where none will transfer to a
finger when tested. The amount of time that this will
take will vary, depending upon the temperature of the
workshop and the amount of catalyst added. Remember
that gel remains tacky to the touch, and doesn't dry hard
on the exposed side; the material is dry when none comes
away onto a testing digit.

Whilst waiting for the gel to dry, you should have been
busying yourself cutting whatever matting you will need
— which means enough to cover your intended area
twice. Ideally, this should consist of two sheets of equal
size. Should you be making up the lamination from
pieces of matting, ensure that the pieces are all torn,
rather than cut, on each edge. This will enable the pieces
to mesh neatly into each other.

You should also have been preparing the lay-up resin
by adding the correct amount of pigment tint; using a
clear resin to back up a tinted gel-coat will result in a
patchy finish on the sheet surface. As a guide to resin
quantities, a square metre of 450g matting will require
750g of resin, which means that two layers will require
double that amount. The ideal receptacle for mixing
such an amount is the bottom half of an empty plastic
one-gallon bottle, thoroughly washed and dried. Do not
use acetone to wash it out, though — the solvent will
melt straight through the plastic.

Add the catalyst to the resin, and mix it properly.
Using a brush or paint roller (the choice is yours), paint a
wet coat of lay-up resin onto the waiting gel-coat. Now
drape your first piece of matting over this, and tamp it
down using the well-wetted brush end-on (trying brush

A small piece of flat sheet being laid up. Once the gel-coat has been applied and allowed to dry to the point where, although still tacky to touch, it won't come off onto a prodding finger, the first coat of lay-up resin is applied, followed by a piece of matting.

Keep the brush loaded with resin and use it end-on, with a stippling rather than a painting action, to avoid dragging the mat out into separate strands.

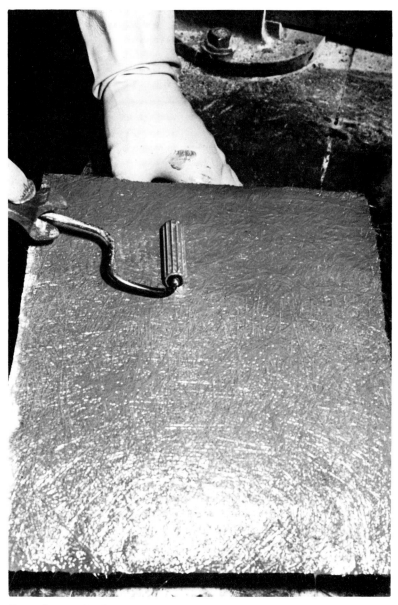

Once the required number of layers of matting have been applied and are thoroughly wet (with no dry areas, which show as silvery-grey), roll out the air bubbles with a paddle or disc roller. This will also help the layers of mat to integrate together.

strokes will only succeed in wrecking the matting) or the similarly saturated roller. The object of the exercise is to saturate the matting. When I first started to laminate, I thought that my tutor Ian was being particularly insulting, calling me a moron. It turned out that he was simply telling me to apply more resin to soak the matting properly. . . .

If you are using smallish pieces of matting, overlap each previous piece by an inch or so to ensure total coverage of the gel. If you are using a single piece, this problem will not arise. What will probably start to happen is that a few air bubbles will appear. Don't worry about them; a few light strokes with your paddle roller will soon sort out that problem, after the next layer of mat has been applied.

To apply the second layer of matting, simply repeat the previous process. Again, take care to ensure that the matting is thoroughly wetted-out — any dry areas will show as silvery highlights. Naturally, there will be no need to put a paint coat on first, prior to draping the second layer of matting, as the first will be wet enough to take the second.

Once you have applied both layers of matting, take your paddle roller, and work systematically from one end of your lamination to the other in an effort to remove all air bubbles. Do not apply too much pressure, as this will stretch the matting overmuch. Work towards an outside edge, the one nearest to the air bubble.

Once you are satisfied that no air remains in the lamination, you can brush out your mixing pot so that all that remains in it is a thin layer of resin (this can be cracked out once it has cured, leaving the pot ready for re-use) and clean out your brush and rollers.

The whole process should not have taken more than ten minutes, which is well within the working time of the resin. However, should you have been delayed for some reason and found that the mix has gone off during the process, roller down the part of the job so far completed,

This simple air duct, intended to feed air from a bonnet-mounted scoop into the carburettor, is just one example of the many applications for flat glassfibre sheet. It was fastened together with a single layer of resined tissue inside and out, giving a smooth, tidy finish.

and clean off the tools before making up a fresh mix and continuing where you left off. There is no need to wait for the already-laid resin to dry off, as it will be unaffected by a new batch being applied over it.

The lamination should now be left to cure for several hours — removing it from the mould at an earlier stage may result in some warpage, as flat sheet has little inherent structural rigidity. Once it has hardened, it can be prised away from the board which acted as its mould, and the smaller the lamination the easier this will be.

Start by prising up one corner, using a thin piece of plastic (such as that supplied with a tin of body filler) or a fine metal scraper. Once you have raised one corner slightly, use a narrow strip of hardboard, smooth side up, and press this between the lamination and the mould, leaving it in place whilst you work progressively along the edge, using first your piece of plastic, and then another piece of hardboard. With luck, the lamination should spring from the board quite soon. On occasion stubbornness will set in, and the only answer here is to have pieces of hardboard on either side of the sheet, and to use them as levers to prise the pieces apart.

Once separated from its former, the sheet of laminate should be left flat for 24 hours before being touched again, which will allow it sufficient time to harden. Once completely hard, it can be cut with an electric jigsaw to whatever shape you require, and permanently bonded to other pieces cut from the same material by using resin and matting.

CHAPTER 16

REPLICA PANELS

There comes a time when steel just will not do any more. Perhaps because original panels are no longer available, or maybe because metal is too heavy and the lightness of a GRP lamination is sought, you are one day overwhelmed by a desire to produce copies of an existing steel wing, bonnet, bootlid or whatever. If the previous project, flat sheeting, was simplicity itself, then producing copies of complex-shaped car body panels is the opposite — the task can vary from merely difficult to downright near-impossibility. But don't let that put you off — it can be done!

The first rule is that a copy will only be as good as the original from which the mould was made; if there are ripples, creases or other irregularities on the original, then they will show up equally prominently on the copy. So the first move is to get the original panel into shape. Almost invariably, body repairs are best done with the panel in place on the car. This will ensure that the panel is kept in shape; wings in particular are prone to twisting once removed from a car. Were you to be repairing the original panel, you could well shy away from body filler because of its excess weight. Such considerations need not be taken into account when repairing ready to produce copies, as the weight of the original panel will be immaterial.

A complete Mini front end. Because there are no inverse curves, this can be moulded in one piece as it will spring from its mould easily.

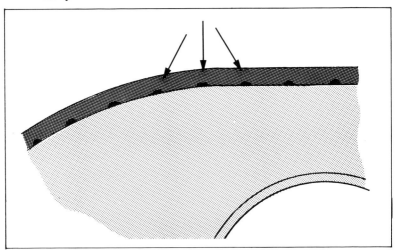

Where necessary, a panel can be split-moulded. Affix a strip of waxed-and-PVA'd hardboard to the split line with blobs of filler (arrowed) and lay up one side of the mould onto the treated splitter. Once cured, remove the splitter and filler, treat the flange which has just been formed with release agents, and trim of the excess material. The other side of the mould can then be made, running up the initial flange to form a second one. When the mould is ready to laminate a copy from, the two sides can be bolted together.

So you can go to it, and use as much body filler as you like, in an effort to recreate the original contours of the panel. Once you are totally satisfied that the shape of the panel is exactly as it should be, the mould can be made from it.

A gel-coat will be the first part of the process, and because this will need to release from the panel, it is necessary to use an isolator prior to the release wax and PVA — otherwise, the gel could well stick to the original panel. Strand Glassfibre produce an excellent product for this purpose, which they describe as Release Agent No 1. This is a compound of cellulose acetate, which effectively seals any porous surfaces. To be on the safe side, apply several coats of this, brushed on lightly and allowed to air dry between coats. The panel should then be waxed, given some six layers in the manner prescribed earlier in the book, whereby each layer is applied, and then buffed off before the next layer is added. Once

This bolt-together mould for TVR's roadster bodyshell is set into a steel frame, to ensure rigidity and durability. For most DIY moulds, it will suffice to use strips of wood.

the final layer of wax has been buffed off, a thin coat of PVA release agent can be applied, and left to dry.

The next problem to be attended to is that of separating the eventual mould from the original. Depending upon the shape of the wing, bonnet or whatever, it may be that a one-piece mould is feasible, and that the two pieces, former and mould, can be separated from each other without difficulty. On the other hand, a panel which has a number of complex curves may require the mould to be made up of several sections which bolt together in use and can then be separated to remove the mould from the former and again, later, to allow the resultant moulding to escape. Should you be intending to make a one-piece front end for a car, then such a mould will be almost unavoidable.

The joint lines for the mould should be decided before the gel-coat is applied, so that any dividers can be positioned. Only when you are ready to make the mould should you start to mix up a batch of resin. It makes sense to colour the mould surfacing gel in a dark colour, as any irregularities will then show up once the former

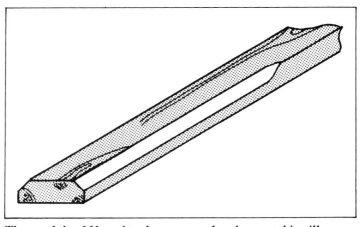

The wood should have its edges removed as shown — this will ensure that the matting does not have to make a sharp right-angle. Use your angle grinder with a sanding disc to remove the edge — this takes a matter of moments, and is quicker than trying to whittle away at the wood with a knife.

panel has been removed. Having tinted your gel, add the catalyst, and apply a thin coat to the former panel. Aim to keep to the industry norm of 0.015in (0.4mm) and ensure that there are no excessive build-ups along the edges or in the corners of the panel.

Once the resin has dried to the point where none will transfer to a testing finger (always test on an area that will be hidden from view on the finished panel, unless you want the world to be able to see your fingerprints immortalized in the centre of a wing top, or wherever) you can start to laminate the mould. Always bear in mind that matting will not go through a 90° bend, and that it will be necessary to lay cut edges neatly into an inside angle, or to drape tissue strip over an outside corner. This was detailed in the section on matting, Chapter 7. Using a mixture of tinted lay-up resin and catalyst, paint

The first part of the process is to prepare the mould surface by waxing it and applying a coat of PVA release agent. Once this has been done, cut to size the required number of pieces of mat, ready for use.

over the gelled area completely before applying any matting.

Now lay on your first piece of mat, using the normal 450g weight. Start from the edge of the mould, using a cut edge on the outside, and torn edges on the inside. Overlap the edge of the former by at least an inch, to ensure that a sufficient thickness of mat is covering the entire former. Overlap the torn edge of your next piece onto the piece already laid down by an inch, making sure that each piece is thoroughly wetted out before the next piece is applied. For most smaller panels, the best tool to use to apply resin is a paintbrush, and this should be used as a stipple, rather than trying to paint with it. This will avoid any undue stretching of the matting. As matting will not drape well over compound curves (where the panel curves in more than one direction at a time) use small enough pieces of mat to ensure that you are not expecting the material to do something that it won't. Remember at all times that the gel-coat must be completely covered by wetted-out mat.

Once you have completely covered the former with resin and mat, you can start to apply the next layer. Again keep your brush wet, and ensure that the matting is saturated. When you have got two layers on the former, and are sure that the overlap is of double strength all around the edges, take a paddle roller and work outwards to rid the lamination of any air bubbles. Use a disc roller to get into corners and ensure a total bond between matting and gel-coat. Now leave the lamination to dry, and clean off the tools and mixing pot that you used.

The lamination should be left for at least 24 hours to cure completely before proceeding with the next stage of adding the stiffeners and carrying frame. The reason for the delay is that if stiffening is added to the moulding whilst the resin is still 'green', or partially cured, the shape of the mould reinforcement strips will be carried through to the front of the lamination.

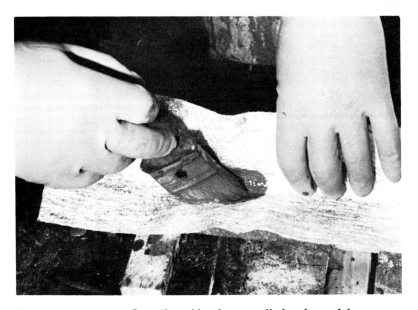

This is a wing spacer. Once the gel has been applied and cured, lay-up resin can be applied, followed by the first piece of matting. Resin is tamped, rather than brushed, over the matting to avoid separation of the strands.

The second layer of matting is wetted out, the brush again being used as a stipple.

So the following day, you return to the workshop and commence adding sufficient stiffening to the mould to ensure that it will keep its shape properly, and not distort. The ideal material to use for this task is one of the few products used in glassfibre lamination that grows on trees — wood. Most timber yards stock some ultra-cheap battening used in roofing (known, appropriately enough, as slate batten) and this is ideal. Using your angle grinder, radius two of the edges on one of the flat faces. Now cut lengths of the wood which will fit the mould, and add strength both along the mould and across it. Depending upon the complexity of the panel shape, these can be as few as three or four pieces, or as many as a dozen. These should be laid with their bevelled edges upwards, and before being positioned should have their ends radiused.

These can now be attached to the moulding, using body filler to tack them into place prior to affixing them permanently with resin and matting, which should be applied as previously. Most professional laminators will at this stage add a set of support legs which will serve to hold the mould either flat or on end at the stage where a copy is being laid up in the mould. A mould which is unsteady or falls over will hardly help you to produce a good result.

Once the stiffeners have been added, lay up another two layers of matting — remember that rigidity is more important than lightness in the case of a mould — and again leave the moulding overnight to harden. Needless to say, the matting should have been rolled out to remove any air bubbles, and the tools should have been washed out after use.

Now is the time to spring the former from the mould. This is best done using a selection of pieces of hard-board, which are prised between the mould and the former. If the former doesn't spring easily from the mould, which it should if you have worked system-atically around the edges with the pieces of hardboard,

Whilst it is true that matting will not easily adopt compound curvatures, it can be made to stretch enough to fit this kind of shape — once wet enough, it will press down into the mould.

The overlap of cut edges can be seen here — this ensures that there is complete coverage of the mould by both layers of matting.

turn the whole caboodle over, and using a plastic-faced mallet, tap over all of the surface of the back of the mould. Localized shock like this should free the former. If it doesn't, keep trying with pieces of hardboard strip until it does — and tell yourself that you will try harder with the release agents next time. . . .

Now the mould can be washed out with a solution of warm soapy water to remove the residue of PVA, and dried off thoroughly. Once dry, the mould can be prepared by waxing it. A new mould needs at least a half-dozen coats of wax, each one being left for a few minutes, then buffed off. To get a really good covering of wax, it pays to leave the mould between coats for a while — anything from a half hour to an hour is about right. Prior to the waxing process, you can inspect the mould carefully to ensure that all is as it should be. If it isn't, there could be a number of reasons; either the former wasn't properly prepared, or the lamination process was not carried out correctly. Check out the table of technical problems at the back of the book to find out how to overcome whatever is wrong with your mould.

Assuming that all is well, you may continue the process by painting on a thin coat of PVA, allowing it to air dry, and then painting on a thin coating of gel, tinted to whatever shade you require the finished product to be (and preferably a different colour to the mould surface, so that you can tell what is fresh gel and what isn't) and catalysed in the correct proportion.

The process is then continued, laying up two thicknesses of glassfibre matting with a pre-tinted and catalysed resin, and rolling out any air bubbles. As with the mould-making process, run past the edge of the mould line with both layers of mat, cut edges outwards, to ensure adequate mat coverage. After the resin has partly cured, that is when it is air-dry but still 'green', the area of matting that has run over the edge of the mould can be trimmed back to the mould edge, using a sharp knife. The lamination should then be left in the

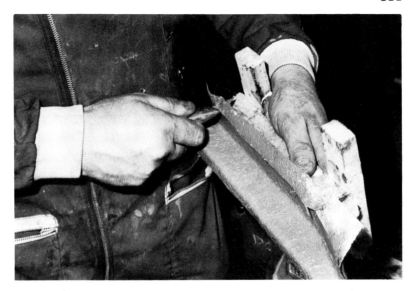

Trimming off the edge can be done either at the 'green' stage, using a knife . . .

. . . or at the cured stage, using a cutting disc in an angle grinder. Always ensure that the disc cuts down into the gel-coat, rather than up through it — this will avoid the gel-coat splintering.

The edge of the mould line can be seen clearly here; trim off the waste edge of material with a cutting disc.

mould until it has hardened properly.

Using the same technique as detailed previously, the copy can be sprung from the mould once completely cured — which should be a couple of hours after lamination has been completed. The reason for using pieces of hardboard, should you be keen to know, is because this material is softer than the gel-coat of a moulding — which means that it will not damage the new panel you have just made. As previously, if the copy is being stubborn, turn the mould over and tap it all over with a soft mallet. This should do the trick.

Most car wings are made in two pieces, the outer section which is on show to the world, and a second section which is attached on the inside, and serves to space the wing out from the inner wing. Quite often, this spacer piece also serves as a mounting for the retaining bolts. On a steel wing, these two pieces will be welded together, and any retaining bolts will either take the form of studs which are affixed to the wing and pass through to the side section of the bulkhead, or bolts which go from inside the car and affix to pre-threaded and reinforced washers attached to the wing spacer.

Were it not for some superb little gadgets known as Bighead Fastenings, recreating the fixing points on a replicated GRP wing could be something of a problem. As it is, all that needs to be done is for holes to be drilled in the spacer panel, and the correct type of Bighead fastener passed through it. The fastener is then bonded to the back of the panel using a small piece of matting and catalysed resin. There are several hundred different sizes of threaded fastener produced by Bighead, and the company also supply a range of captive nuts attached to Bighead plates. The plates themselves are perforated, to ensure a good, permanent bond to the moulding.

To affix a spacer panel to the back of the wing, it is necessary to first trim the edges of both items. This is easiest done with an angle grinder fitted with a sanding disc. Work gently into the edge of the material, taking care not to cut into the material inside the trim-off line that will be formed by the gel-coat of the original mould and which will show on the edge of any copies.

Once both pieces have been trimmed, mix up a small amount of body filler, suitably catalysed, and spread this along the face of the spacer that will mate to the wing. Position the spacer, and use several G-clamps to hold the two pieces together until the filler has set. Any excess filler which is squeezed out from between the two faces should be removed before it has hardened. Once the clamps have been removed, the filler can be reinforced by laminating layers of matting into place, using catalysed lay-up resin.

If you have produced a replica of a bonnet or bootlid, particularly a lightweight racing panel which is made up of only two layers of matting, you will be risking the centre of the panel sagging unless provision is made for some form of reinforcement. With a bonnet for racing

Some of the immense range of Bighead fasteners which are ideal for affixing removable panels. The perforated flanges allow the fasteners to be laminated securely into a moulding.

purposes, it is quite likely that some form of air induction scoop will be added, and this may well add enough rigidity to the panel. It is, however, better to be safe than sorry with such matters, and for that reason I would most strongly recommend that you provide a degree of reinforcement anyway — ensuring that you are not passing into the area that will be taken up by your airscoop.

Paper rope is just about ideal as a means of obtaining stiffening on a large panel. Whilst it has no intrinsic strength, once it has been laminated over it adds a massive amount of additional rigidity to a panel. There are a number of right and wrong ways of going about adding stiffness to a panel; having devised a suitable pattern, arrange your strips of paper rope over the inside of the panel before it has been removed from the mould (thus ensuring that it is holding to its intended shape) but after the lamination has been left to cure for 24 hours. That way, lines caused by the shrinkage of the reinforcing strips will not be seen coming through the layers of matting once the panel is affixed to the car.

The strips of paper rope can be glued to the inside of the panel using blobs of catalysed body filler every few inches. Once the filler has hardened (again, as with fixing

One way of fixing a lightweight panel to a car is to use a pit pin. The pin is attached to the lower panel of the car, and passes through the lightweight panel. The clip then passes through the pin and holds the panel down.

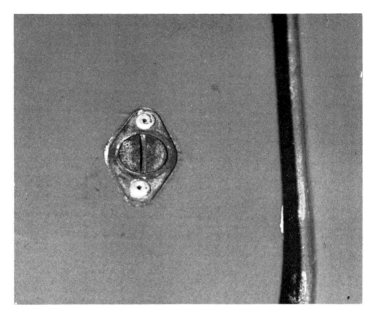

A Dzus quarter-turn fastener. The upper part of the clip is attached to the lightweight panel, usually with a pair of blind rivets . . .

the two parts of a wing together, excess material should be removed before it cures), the rope can then be laminated onto the panel permanently, using cut strips of matting which will adhere to the panel by a couple of inches on either side of the rope. Two layers should be perfectly adequate to strengthen the panel. Apply the matting in the usual way, ensuring that your brush is thoroughly wet, and that the paper rope is well soaked in resin before the first layer is applied. Leave the panel in the mould for a further 24 hours after adding the stiffeners to ensure that distortion will not set in.

The biggest problem that tends to rear its ugly head with replacement GRP bonnets and bootlids is that of affixing them to the car. Every case is different, but there are a number of methods of fixing which may be of help. The first of these is to laminate in place suitably-sized pieces of inch-thick timber (as distinct from chipboard, which would tend to separate) onto which can be affixed the various bits of hardware. These should be bonded to the panel whilst it is still in the mould, and the edges of the wood should be bevelled before being laminated over with two layers of matting.

Whilst bonding in a selection of pieces of timber offers a great deal of adaptability, a far more precise method of fixing hinges would be to incorporate Bighead fasteners onto the edge of the panel, positioned to relate to the

...whilst the lower part of the clip which holds the locating spring is attached to the carrying panel.

hinges already affixed to the bulkhead or back valance of the car. As with wing fitments, the type of fastener used can be either male or female, to suit the particular installation. A third, and still easier, option is to use pit pins or Dzus fasteners. I have chosen this method of fixing for the bonnet and bootlid on my own drag racer 'The Menace', which has enabled me to make further weight savings on the car. I have used Dzus quarter-turn fasteners, one to each corner of the panel, and this enables me to remove the panel in its entirety. This is fine for racing purposes, but it would be a pain on a street-driven car, where it is far more convenient to have a hinged cover.

Locking the new, lightweight panels may become something of a problem, if you are unable to install the original equipment. Fortunately, a number of the more enlightened security companies have attended to the problems, and there are a number of products by firms such as Yale and Lander which can be easily adapted for use on bonnets and bootlids. A visit to a locksmith (ideally before you start to install the panel) will enable you to obtain a suitable lock mechanism.

CHAPTER 17

SPOILERS

It appears that even with the plethora of bolt-on spoilers that are available, there are still cars that remain not catered for. There is also the fact that whilst there are often several different designs of spoiler available for a particular car, none of them may quite meet the requirements of the would-be modifier. The only option in either case is to build up a spoiler from scratch.

Back in the late 1970s, I spent quite some time talking to the extremely knowledgeable head of design at Vauxhall, Wayne Cherry. In addition to styling such stunning machines as the stillborn Equus project, the affable American and his team were also involved in restyling several of the production models in the GM range. These included the Black Magic Chevette and the sensational Silver Aero, which later became a production reality (in toned-down form) in the Manta series.

Wayne's method of restyling a car was to make up a dummy spoiler, using cardboard, modelling clay, foam, wire and tape — the choice of material used being governed by the complexity of the selected design. Then he and his team would walk away from the vehicle, and look at it subjectively, asking themselves such questions as 'Does it suit the car. .? Is the design balanced. .? does it look right. .?' Only when they were satisfied with the design, which often meant making a few changes here

The Equus project, with its glassfibre bodyshell, which regrettably never made it into production, was the product of Wayne Cherry's styling team at Vauxhall.

A definitive example of the success of well-designed spoilers improving the looks (and performance, in this case) of an otherwise mundane car was the Black Magic version of the Chevette.

Taking a production Sportshatch version of the Cavalier and adding a beautifully-balanced set of skirts and spoilers was how Vauxhall arrived at the Silver Aero — forerunner in style of the current Opel Monza model.

and there, and almost invariably adding a rear spoiler in order to balance the car's appearance, would they go a stage further and produce glassfibre replicas of the dummy panels.

Such a method involves a lot of time, and even more thought. They quite often would have started by sketching out the car's basic shape on paper, and then adding spoilers to the drawing, and this makes sense for the amateur to try. If your artistic capabilities are strictly limited, you could trace over photographs of the car to achieve your basic sketch. Only when you are totally happy with your mock-ups should you start to make a former from which to produce the finished product.

There are several methods of fabricating a former, and none of them is particularly easy or quick. Metal brake piping is an extremely useful material to have handy as it can be easily bent to shape, and can be joined together by brazing or even soldering. The ends can also be flattened

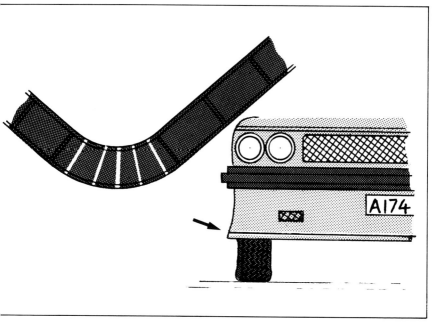

Taking a basic framework of wire or rod and then cladding it with pieces of card is an ideal way of making a former upon which to work. The arrow shows where a keyline can be painted to achieve a visual impression of a spoiler lower than is actually practicable.

out and drilled through in order to pop-rivet them to the bodywork. A less versatile, but cheaper alternative would be to use baling wire, which is available from any horticultural dealer — its intended application is for holding bales of hay together down on the farm. Welding rod is another very useful material for this purpose as it is so easy to join together.

Use the pipe or wire to make up the basic shape of the spoiler, fixing the framework to the car to ensure accuracy of fit. As with the mock-up, keep checking that everything is visually effective — and also that the complete framework is completely symmetrical. Before affixing one piece of tube to another, measure that it is equally positioned at each end. Believe me, nothing looks more half-cocked than an out-of-line spoiler.

Once your basic framework is together and in place,

you can start to cover it over. If your chosen design is simple, with no compound curves, glassfibre sheet, card, or aluminium are about ideal. For external curves, thin strips are the way to cover the framework. For a more complex shape, sheet foam is the ideal material to use. This can be affixed to the framework using lay-up resin (having first degreased the metal with an acetone-soaked rag) and subsequently shaped using a Surform plane.

What happens from here depends upon your future plans: if you are intending to make this a one-off exercise you can make the former a permanent fixture, whilst if you are intending to make more than one spoiler (perhaps for sale to other club members, friends, or whatever — which could be a good way of recouping your expenses) then you should make a mould from the former, which will enable you to spring copies as and when you please.

To turn the former into a permanent addition, start by tearing strips of matting, this time with a weight of 300g, rather than the more normal 450g. The strips should be no wider than the depth of the spoiler, and of a manageable length — about eighteen inches by four inches should be about right for the main area of the typical front spoiler, and a few small pieces, again with torn rather than cut edges, will come in handy for covering the curves. Mix a pot of lay-up resin, tinting it in the nearest shade that you can obtain to that of your vehicle. Now catalyse the mix to suit conditions (remembering never to exceed 3%) and paint a coat of resin over the spoiler and over an inch-wide strip of the bodywork around its edges. It ought to go without saying that the surrounding bodywork should have been degreased before starting the project.

Lay your first piece of matting over the former, and wet it out using your brush as a stipple, to avoid stretching the mat. Now extend from that piece, overlapping by an inch and wetting each subsequent piece thoroughly, taking care to ensure even coverage of

By replacing the original heavy steel bootlid on his Vauxhall racer with a two-ply glassfibre item, Kurt Hinchcliffe managed to save a vast amount of weight and incorporate a rear spoiler at the same time.

the former. Where the spoiler joins the bodywork, take your first layer of matting an inch onto the original panel, which will serve to hold the assembly in place permanently. Apply a second layer of matting, but this time use a cut edge where the spoiler meets the body panel. Any low-spots (not uncommon, especially where external curves are being covered) can be raised by applying additional matting. Now roller out any air bubbles using a paddle roller and disc roller, and leave the lamination to cure. Occupy yourself for a few minutes of this time by cleaning out your pot and washing your tools.

It is advisable to leave the lamination overnight before carrying out the next stage of the process, which is to sand down the surface to a reasonably smooth finish. Once this has been done, the surface can be inspected, and any remedial work (such as filling in any air holes that are discovered, levelling any low spots, and so forth) carried out. Once you are satisfied with the condition of the moulding, you can continue by applying a single layer of surfacing tissue. This should be applied in as large a piece as possible. Once the main piece is on, add extra pieces as necessary, again using torn, rather than cut, edges and overlapping slightly onto the previous piece. Run the tissue over the strip of matting that has been laid onto the body panel. Roller out the tissue, and leave it to cure properly.

From here to achieving a perfect surface is a matter of yet more elbow grease, using several coats of high-build spray primer at a time, and sanding them down until the surface is totally smooth and ready for painting. This may take several days, so be warned. Bear in mind at all times that the finished coat of body colour will highlight any undulations in the surface of your new spoilers. For this reason most professional body shops apply a guide coat of black paint before applying any colour — a light sanding back of the guide coat will show any ripples up before it is too late.

If you have decided to produce a mould from which to make copies (there are a number of advantages to doing it this way, such as keeping the weight of the fitted spoiler down, and also the adaptability which will allow you to replace your spoiler completely should it ever get damaged, as happens so often with racing machinery) the process is basically similar, but with a few essential differences.

Start by degreasing the former as previously, then apply a copious amount of tape over the bodywork surrounding the spoiler — this time, we don't want any resin to apply itself to the car bodywork. The ideal tape to use for this purpose is Race Tape. This is available from any good race-equipment supplier in 2-inch wide rolls, and costs about £4.50 at 1986 prices. Now carry out the lamination process as for the previous exercise —

but this time use a cut edge abutting the bodywork on both layers. Follow the same routine of sanding, layering with surfacing tissue, and smoothing out the surface until you are positive that the finish is perfect.

Once there, you will need to seal and isolate the surface before proceeding further. This is easiest to achieve by applying several coats of Strand Glassfibre's No 1 release agent. Once this has dried, the spoiler should be given six successive coats of wax, each being left for ten minutes before buffing off and then left for a further half-hour before applying the next coat. Finally, an application of PVA release agent will facilitate the subsequent moulding's easy release. The masking tape should be removed from the bodywork at this stage, and the area given a similar releasing agent treatment to the spoiler.

Rather than use a boot-mounted aerofoil, TVR have developed this undertray as a means of holding the rear end of their superb 350i to the ground at high speed, an idea worth considering for other cars.

To achieve the excellent finish of their cars, TVR spend time working on the bare shells with high-build primer, a product midway between a filler and an undercoat, which eliminates any tiny indentations.

Using lay-up resin and 450g matting, apply two layers to the former, overlapping onto the bodywork by about two inches. Whereas on the previous project it would be advisable to laminate on both front and back of the spoiler, there is no reason to laminate both sides of a front spoiler when the object of the exercise is to produce a mould from which to spring copies. Instead, simply overlap the bottom edge of the spoiler by an inch or so. As the natural tendency of the matting will be to drop downwards, you may have to keep re-tamping the bottom of the matting until it holds the desired shape.

Once the lamination process is finished, leave the car for 24 hours to ensure that the resin cures properly before proceeding further. On your return to the vehicle, you should apply some stiffening to the lamination by using strips of paper rope or pieces of 1in × 1in wood which have had their outer corners radiused. These should be laid in both directions to ensure equal reinforcement, and glued into place using body filler. Once the filler has hardened the stiffeners can be laminated over with two layers of matting, and again left overnight to cure. The following day, release the lamination from the former by first tapping it all over with a soft mallet, and then prising between the body-work and the mould with a selection of pieces of hardboard strip. Once the mould is free of the former, it can be washed out with lukewarm soapy water to remove all traces of PVA, and inspected closely. Provided all is well, the former can then be removed from the car bodyshell and disposed of. The only damage to the bodyshell should be the odd hole where pop-rivets had lived whilst holding the former in place — and those will be covered by the spoiler that you are about to make.

The mould should now be trimmed, prior to preparing it for copying from. Quite where you trim it to is really up to you, but as a guide I would recommend that the flange which will attach the spoiler to the car should be about 1 ½in wide and run the full width of the spoiler. At the bottom of the spoiler, a half-inch past the point where the glassfibre wraps under the front should be about right. Cutting the excess material off the mould is easiest achieved with a diamond-tip cutting wheel on an angle grinder, but should you not possess one of those, an electric jigsaw would suffice. Whichever method of cutting you choose, great care should be taken to ensure that the gel-coat is not damaged by the cutting action. If using a cutting disc, ensure that the direction of rotation of the disc takes the edge into the gel-coat first, and then on into the laminate. With a jigsaw, the blade is designed to cut on the up stroke, and so cutting should be undertaken from the laminate side of the mould. Failure to observe either of these rules will almost invariably result in the gel cracking away from the edge in great

As this shot shows, the pay-off for such work is a smooth and even set of panels, with no trace of the various mould joint lines. Put a similar degree of effort into your mouldings and the results will be equally worthwhile.

chunks, so beware.

Once the mould has been trimmed, it can be prepared in the usual manner, by applying six coats of wax, followed by a thin coat of PVA release agent. The copies can then be made by painting on a layer of gel-coat, allowing it to dry, and then following it with a coat of lay-up resin, a layer of matting, and so forth. Two layers of 450g matting will be fine for the bulk of the lamination, but add a third layer on the edges for strength. Ensure that the matting which runs off the edge of the mould has a cut edge, and that each layer does overlap the edge of the mould. Roller out the air bubbles, and leave the lamination to dry out overnight before springing it free of the mould using strips of hardboard, as previously described.

A typical front spoiler, this TVR item incorporates a pair of driving lamps and the cooling air intake.

All that then remains is to trim the panel and fit it to the car. Using a cutting disc or jigsaw as previously, cut back the excess material, and finish off by sanding the edges smooth. At the same time flatten off any whiskers of matting that are emerging from the surface of the laminate, using coarse abrasive paper. Affixing the spoiler is then a simple matter of drilled holes with large self-tapping screws, blind rivets, or small nuts and bolts. Whichever of the three fixing methods you choose, it is advisable to use washers against the face of the moulding, to spread the load slightly. Ensure that the holes in the GRP are slightly oversize to avoid straining the gel-coat surface.

Whilst all of the preceding has been primarily concerned with front spoilers, many of the techniques apply equally to rear spoilers. Where there are substantial differences are with such issues as fixing the spoiler to the bodywork, making the spoiler in two halves, and dealing with the problem of a sagging spoiler.

Taking these one at a time, a good starting point is the problem of fixing the spoiler to the car. Here, at the back of the car, the spoiler can rarely be affixed by a flange, as is usual at the front. Instead, it is possible to laminate a piece of wood into the bottom of the spoiler, which can be screwed into from the inside of the bootlid.

When it comes to making a spoiler in two halves, the thing to do is to pick a suitable split line, and then affix strips of hardboard around the edges of the former. These will then form flanges on the mould which will in turn allow the subsequent lamination to be made in two halves which can then be joined together. The halves can be permanently attached to each other by the strategic use of lay-up resin, the two pieces being clamped together until the curing process is complete.

The third problem I mentioned, that of the centre of the spoiler sagging, is a common one — just look at most of the Escort aftermarket GRP spoilers if you do not believe me. . . . Yet for all of its proliferation, the problem is a surprisingly easy one to overcome; before either laminating on the bottom of the spoiler, or by drilling a 1in diameter hole which can later be blanked over, pour in a sufficient quantity of polyurethane foam mix immediately after combining the two constituents.

Even a complex shape such as this Porsche 911 whale-tail spoiler can be moulded in glassfibre. The mould would need to be a splitter, separating into two or more parts to facilitate release of the finished copy.

This will enlarge to fill the cavity, and will add a staggering degree of strength. Always wear a breathing mask when carrying out this process, as the gases given off by the foam during its expansion process are poisonous — to about the same degree as the average Black Mamba's bite.

As a short cut, it is tempting to take an existing spoiler for another make or model of car and modify it. Before you start to do this, a word of warning; many of the aftermarket panels available for cars are produced in ABS plastic, injection-moulded to shape. This has been known to react with resin and melt away to nothing but a gooey mess of molten material. If you have no other choice but to use this plastic as a former, it is necessary to isolate it totally from the resin by using a purpose-made primer. Consult your local trade car paint supplier about the problem, and see what primer they can supply for this purpose.

The last piece of advice I can offer on the subject of spoilers concerns those for the front of the car. Whilst copying the ultra-low, racetrack style can make your car look absolutely tremendous, it will only take a piece of careless kerbside parking or hitting a deep pothole to wreck the newest addition to your car. If you really are serious about having a ground-hugging spoiler, make the part in glass to a reasonable depth, and then use rubber strip to take it lower to Mother Earth. Or you could make the spoiler to an acceptable drop which is not as vulnerable as a ground-hugger, and create a visual trick by applying a keyline around it, about an inch from the bottom, in a contrasting colour. This gives the effect of lowering the car, but without actually doing so. It works for Wayne Cherry and the team at General Motors, so why shouldn't it work for you. . . ?

CHAPTER 18

AIR INTAKES

Whether for serious technical reasons or visual effect, many modified cars show some form of air intake somewhere on their bodyshells. Having either an intake or escape for the engine bay is a favourite, followed closely by ducts which are intended to feed cooling air to the brakes.

There are quite a number of proprietary bonnet scoops and bulges available in GRP, and it may well prove most cost-effective to purchase one (or several, if you are that way inclined) of these and to attach it to the car in either standard form, or perhaps with your own modifications added.

Should you be unable to find a suitable existing scoop (check such publications as *Street Machine*, *Custom Car*, *Performance Ford* and *Cars & Car Conversions* for advertisers) then you are, once again, out on your own. The first move is to decide quite what you want; bear in mind that whilst a scoop which rises mightily above the bonnet may look magnificent on a drag-racing door-slammer, transplanting the same design to a road car may well reduce visibility through the screen by a quite marked amount. If you are looking to extract hot air from the engine compartments, a pair of NACA ducts let into the bonnet will do the job admirably, allowing egress to hot air whilst the car is stationary, and forcing

Prominent on the bonnet of this Porsche 924 Turbo is a NACA duct air intake. A similar device will work on most cars as an aid to underbonnet cooling and is simple to construct.

Photo: Porsche Cars (GB) Ltd.

cool air into the underbonnet space when the machine is on the move. These are surprisingly simple to make, and to make life even simpler for you, I have provided a template from which you can work. If you are really neat and tidy with an electric jigsaw, you can use the piece which has been cut out of the panel to form the bottom of the intake — but I'm racing ahead a little with that, so let's start at the beginning.

Mark out neatly on your bonnet the positions where you intend to position your ducts, ensuring that they are equally spaced from the edges of the panel, and that they are perfectly aligned with each other. Copy out the template provided in the book onto a piece of paper, and cut it out. Lay it in place on the bonnet, and carefully mark around it with an indelible pen. Now repeat the process on the other side of the bonnet. Drill a pilot hole in the corner of the marked-out area, and insert a hand-gripped hacksaw blade — most modelling shops can

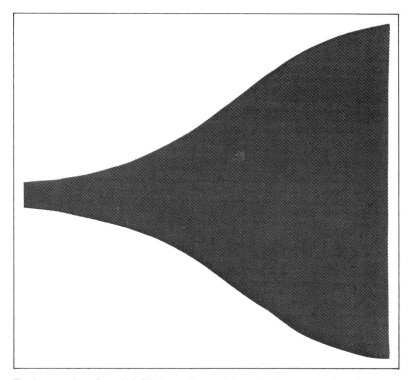

Basic template for a NACA duct. Trace this and enlarge or reduce it to suit your requirements. Originally developed for aircraft use, the distinctive 'curved delta' shape of the NACA duct maximizes air entry while minimizing drag.

supply suitable tools for this purpose. Work steadily and cut out the shape of the duct slowly, avoiding any damage to the gel-coat of your panel. Stop cutting an eighth of an inch short of the pointed end of the duct shape, so that the piece that you have just cut out is still supported, but only just so.

The next part of the process will be made substantially easier if the bonnet is removed from the car. Turn the bonnet over onto its face side (laying it on something soft to avoid scratching) and carefully pull back the open edge of the first duct so that there is a gap of about 1 ¼ in at the trailing edge. You now need to cut a pair of strips of cardboard which will follow the contours of the duct

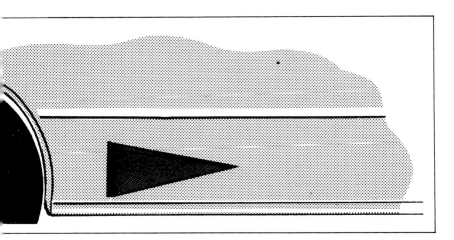

An even simpler intake duct can be made by using a basically triangular layout. This one is fitted in the side of the car as a means of supplying cool air to the rear brakes, or to feed the radiator or oil cooler on a rear-engined car which suffers overheating problems.

sides, and will serve to hold the open edge at the correct height (which will be a drop on the finished bonnet) and taper back to the point where the edge joins the bonnet at the pointed end.

Once the card has been cut and shaped, it should be attached to the bonnet and duct base using adhesive tape strips. Mix a small amount of tinted lay-up resin to the same colour as the bonnet, and catalyse it. Wet out the card thoroughly, and leave it to dry out before proceeding further. This will stiffen it enough to allow the subsequent layers of matting to be applied without distorting the sides.

As soon as the card has dried, mix a fresh batch of catalysed resin, again tinted to the desired shade, and wet out the whole of the duct and an area of several inches on either side of the hole. Using thin strips of 450g matting, starting with a cut edge along the open end of the scoop bottom, gradually layer the matting, using torn edges to overlap the previous piece, until the whole of the assembly has got two layers of matting over it and this extends onto the bonnet underside for a couple of

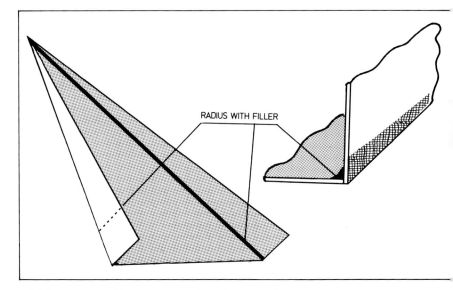

RADIUS WITH FILLER

Whichever type of duct you install, make up wedge shapes to form the sides of the scoop and laminate right over them and onto the original panel. Finish off by radiusing the inside corners neatly with filler.

inches all round. Roll out the air bubbles, clean out your tools and pot, and then repeat the process for the other side of the bonnet.

Once the resin has cured completely, the bonnet can be turned over and the job finished off. Using abrasive paper, smooth out the edges of the cut hole in the bonnet. It is not essential to get a super-smooth finish at this stage, as there remains a little laminating to be done before the project is complete. Mix a small pot of resin to the colour of the bonnet, paint out the inside of the duct, and then, working very gently and using your brush as a stipple, apply a layer of surfacing tissue to the duct. This will considerably smooth out the surface. Once the resin has made its initial curing, any excess tissue can be trimmed off with a sharp knife before leaving the ducts to dry completely. All that then remains is to mask off the area surrounding each duct, apply a high-build primer, and sand it smooth. Once you are satisfied with the

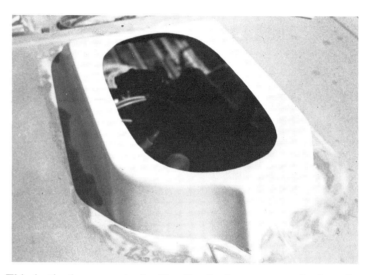

This is the lower part of a Pro-Stock air scoop attached to the lightweight two-ply glassfibre bonnet of Ian Franz's drag racing Marina. The complete assembly is illustrated back in Chapter 11.

finish, a coat of colour can be applied and the job is finished.

Whilst those ducts were specified as a means of reducing underbonnet temperatures, such devices can be equally applied for supplying cooling air to the front brakes of a car by inserting a pair in strategic positions on the front spoiler. The same method is employed, the only difference being that they are scaled down to suit the proportions of the spoiler.

From here, we can progress neatly to external scoops, starting with a pre-purchased item such as the Pro-Stock item shown on Ian Franz's Marina drag racer. This is produced in two parts, the box that forms the top and the bottom section which is first attached to the bonnet. There are two ways of attaching this piece, either having the flange laid on the outside of the bonnet, trimmed back to suit, and then affixed with self-tapping screws or blind rivets, or cutting a hole in the bonnet which is very slightly larger than the scoop base through which the scoop can be passed. The flange is then

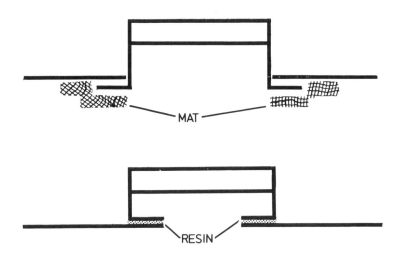

To attach a scoop such as this to the car, we opted to pass it through the bonnet and laminate it into place from beneath, as shown in section (top). Where a ready-made scoop has a reversed flange, bond it to the outside of the panel with resin as shown below. If necessary, back up the resin with self-tapping screws temporarily inserted from beneath until it has cured.

laminated to the underside of the bonnet, and the top section added.

Because the latter method gives a far tidier appearance, we chose that way to affix the scoop. The first move was to mark out the position of the scoop, ensuring that it was not only centred laterally, but was also situated neatly over the carburettor that it was intended to feed with cold air. In order to make the hole through which the scoop would be passing the right size and shape, the base flange of the scoop was first trimmed back to an equal distance from the sides all round. It was then put onto the bonnet, marked around, and then taken off. Then a second line was marked onto the bonnet, inside the original line by the exact width of the flange. After everything had been checked and double-checked, the bonnet was put under the electric jigsaw and the hole cut out. With a little bit of fine adjustment the scoop passed through the bonnet perfectly.

The resin was then mixed, and a double layer of matting strips were laid over the flange and onto the bonnet underside, the air bubbles removed by using a paddle roller, and the assembly left to dry. As I have already mentioned in Chapter 16 on making replacement panels, adding a scoop like this not only ensures that a plentiful supply of cool air is made available, but also that the bonnet is substantially strengthened by the 'triangulation' effect of adding the new shape.

Affixing the upper part of the scoop to the base was a simpler matter of painting a coat of catalysed resin to the surfaces which would mate, and then adding a dozen self-tapping screws (with washers to spread the load) through from the base section into the box base.

In an effort to insulate the carburettor from under-bonnet heat, we decided to make up an air box which would form a duct directly from the scoop into the carburettor. This was a simple proposition, using pieces of flat glassfibre sheet cut to shape, the base being cut out to suit the Holley carburettor's top-plate shape. A strip of steel suitably spaced and drilled took care of holding this in place. Once the shape had been determined, strips of matting were bonded into place on the outside of the box, and then left to cure. A layer of tissue was applied throughout the inside of the box, and the whole thing was finished off with a paint coat of resin tinted in the same red that the car's panels had been moulded from.

A look much-favoured in the halcyon street-racing days was to have the scoop attached to the carburettor of a V8 engine, and poking through a hole in the bonnet. That way, as the engine torque-twisted under power, the scoop would move with it, an effect called the shaker scoop. Making one would be a combination of the scoop and the air box that Ian and I affixed to the Marina. The only problem area is deciding how much space to allow around the scoop — get it too tight a fit and there are problems with the scoop colliding with the bonnet.

Another type of scoop often available is the little one

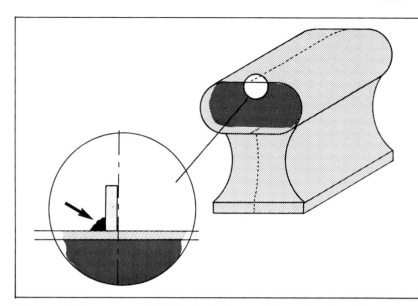

The mould for a scoop of this basic design would need to be split along its length to allow the moulding to come out. A fence of hardboard or glassfibre sheet is first attached to the former with blobs of filler, arrowed. The first side of the mould can then be laid up, with a flange formed against the dividing fence. When curing is complete, the fence is removed, the flange on the first half mould treated with release agents and the second half laid up onto the former and flange. The two halves of the mould are held together by bolts while producing the moulding.

like that attached to the bonnet of my old 100E street-racer. This came with a blanked-off front panel which had to be cut out, and an internal flange. To affix this to the bonnet, the scoop was first positioned in its chosen location, and marked around once all the necessary measurements had been taken to ensure that it was sited squarely on the panel. As with the Pro-Stock scoop, the flange was trimmed to an exact distance from the edge of the scoop, and a similar allowance made on the bonnet. The hole was cut out, and the scoop positioned whilst the minor trimming was attended to.

A layer of resin was then painted onto the two mating surfaces (which had been prepared by rough-sanding them to score the gel-coat) and the scoop held in place by

This little scoop from Fibresports has been moulded to the two-ply bonnet of my own racer, *The Menace*. The front aperture has been cut to provide direct cold air to a four-barrel Holley carburettor.

strategically-positioned self-tapper screws. Again, washers were used on the screws to spread the loading. Once the resin had cured, the edge of the scoop was moulded to the bonnet by using body filler. As the bonnet moulding was done in white, the scoop black and the intended colour of the car still to be decided, the use of filler was no problem, and completely unnoticeable once the car was sprayed. Should your car already be in colour, and you are loathe to respray the panel, an equally neat solution could be to insert a strip of trim bead (from a coachtrimming suppliers) between the scoop and its mounting panel.

Between these three methods, you should be able to fit just about any of the many ready-to-wear scoops and power bulges that are available. What is more, providing that the surface is taken back to bare metal on the areas to be laminated over, the methods will apply as well to steel or aluminium bonnets as to glassfibre ones.

If you are unable to find a suitable scoop already in

production, it will be a matter of making a former to suit your requirements. Start with wood, card, rod or wire, and build up your desired shape in clay, polyurethane foam, or body filler. Once you have arrived at your desired shape and have smoothed it out completely, you will need to make a mould from it, which means that the surface will first have to be sealed properly with several coats of Strand's No 1 release agent. This should then be followed by a series of layers of wax, leaving each for ten minutes between application and buffing, and then a further half-hour before the next coat. Finish the preparation by applying a coat, thinly applied, of PVA release agent.

Prepare a pot of gel-coat, tinting it to whatever shade takes your fancy — so long as it is a different hue from that which your subsequent copy will be. Catalyse this in the correct proportions, and apply a thin layer to the mould — remembering that you should not exceed 0.015in (0.4mm) as anything thicker will lead to gel wrinkling. Once the gel has cured (so that it is still tacky, but will not transfer to an enquiring finger), the lamin-

Another Porsche air intake is the bonnet scoop on the dramatic limited-production 924 Carrera, possible inspiration for your own one-off design easily adaptable to a variety of cars.

Photo: Porsche Cars (GB) Ltd.

ation process can begin. Paint over the entire structure with a catalysed and resin tinted mix, and then start to drape pieces of 450g matting, wetting them through thoroughly by using the brush as a stipple before adding the next piece. Overlap each piece by an inch or so, and use torn edges where pieces join — saving cut edges for the run-off past the edge of the former. Apply two layers of matting, roller out the air bubbles with a paddle or disc roller, and then leave the piece to cure whilst you wash out your tools.

As a scoop is a quite small object, it is highly unlikely that there will be any call for reinforcing strips to be added to the mould. What may be needed is to split the mould into two, or possibly even more, pieces to enable the subsequent copy to be removed from it. This should be done before making the entire piece; insert strips to form flanges at 90° to the mould surface, and lay up the first side of the mould. Subsequent parts can then be moulded onto this, the surface of the flange being treated with release agents before proceeding.

Once the basic mould has been made, which means adding a further two layers of matting to those already laminated, and the whole assembly being left to cure properly (which means overnight), the mould can be sprung from the former by prising strips of hardboard between the two items. As with the previous exercises, a stubborn mould can be released from its former by assisting the hardboard with a few strategic taps from a soft-faced mallet on the back of the lamination.

Once the mould has been made, it should be inspected closely, and prepared for copying from by applying six layers of wax in the manner already described, followed by a thin coating of PVA. It is then a matter of repeating the lamination process by applying a coat of gel, followed once it has cured by two layers of 450g matting. The final copy can be sprung from the mould a couple of hours after lamination is completed, and trimmed off using an angle grinder.

CHAPTER 19

INTERIOR TRIM

Because the originals are either non-existent or totally inadequate, you may have a burning desire to produce replacement trim panels for the inside of your car. These may be to line the inside of the doors, or perhaps as a replacement facia. And you may be wondering how you can produce a grained effect on them.

The first thing to do is to make a former, using whatever materials are most suitable from a list which includes wire, tube, glassfibre sheet, card, timber and sheet polyurethane foam. Once you have established a suitable shape (existing panel sections from other cars may be useful for this, too) the complete assembly should be covered in grained leathercloth, glued into place. This is very much easier said than done, and a tremendous amount of care must be taken if you are to avoid not only wrinkles in the fabric, but also getting glue all over the leathercloth and yourself. A good coachtrimmer will be able to supply you with the ideal adhesives to use and also the leathercloth itself — if you are dealing with compound curves, explain this to the supplier and they will be able to offer you a fabric with the right stretching characteristics.

The surface should then be sealed, using Strand's No 1 release agent. Build up two or three coats applied very thinly, taking great care not to block the grain of the

Grain-effect panels like those seen here on the GTD 40 facia are easy to make, if time consuming.

leathercloth — which would rather defeat the object. Instead of the usual arrangement of using wax on the surface to act as a release agent, sidestep that part of the routine and pass straight on to giving the surface two very thin coats of PVA, again taking great care not to fill the indentations of the grain.

Mix a pot of gel-coat resin, tinting it in a dark colour. Once you have catalysed it, apply a thin coating to the former and leave it until it is cured. Once the surface is tacky but will not come off onto a testing digit, you are ready to commence laminating. Use 300g matting for the first layer, wetting out the gel-coat surface with a mix of lay-up resin tinted to the same shade as the gel-coat, and catalysed to suit conditions. Stipple the surface of the matting with your brush tip, ensuring that each piece is thoroughly wetted-out before adding the next piece. As with any lamination, run off the edge of the mould using a cut edge of matting, but use all torn edges where pieces adjoin each other. Allow a one-inch overlap onto each previous piece. Once the first layer has been applied, you can increase the weight of the matting used to the normal 450g — or apply two further layers of 300g matting. Leave the lamination to cure, and clean off your tools and equipment.

If you are laminating a small item, there should be no need to add any stiffening to the new mould. If the panel is large enough to make flexing or twisting a potential problem, add stiffening by using either strips of wood which have had their outside corners radiused, or

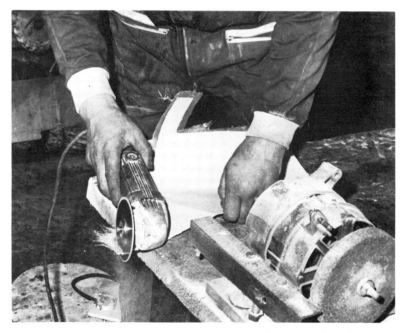

This shape is being produced in single-ply glassfibre as an interior trim panel. After trimming, it will be covered in leathercloth and inserted into the Elan for which it is intended. The combination of its covering and fixing screws mean that there is adequate strength in the single-layer lamination. Stress-bearing pieces should comprise at least two layers of matting.

lengths of paper rope. In either case they can be tacked into place using blobs of catalysed body filler, prior to laminating over them with a couple of further layers of matting. Always leave the mould overnight between initial lay-up and adding the stiffening to ensure that the position of the reinforcements will not show through onto the surface of the mould.

Once the second phase of lamination has been allowed to cure, the pattern can be stripped out from the mould by prising the two pieces apart with a selection of small pieces of hardboard. Because of the minimal use of release agents required with this finish, you may experience some difficulty in achieving this. Tapping over the whole surface of the moulding with a soft-faced mallet is a most worthwhile expedient for solving this problem.

Having got the mould apart from the former, it is time to examine it. Wash out the inside with warm soapy water to remove all traces of PVA, using a small scrubbing brush to ensure that the recesses are completely clear of all traces.

Because the mould shows a reversed, relief version of the finished product, it should be possible to apply several light coats of wax to its surface. This will be a particularly time-consuming process, as it is essential that no lumps of unbuffed wax are attached to the surface of the mould. Once the waxing process is complete, apply a thin coating of PVA, and let it dry.

Mix up a pot of lay-up resin, tinting it to the shade you have selected for your panels — which tends to be black. Once you have catalysed the mix, carefully brush a thin layer onto the surface of the mould. Now lay on a piece of surfacing tissue, shiny side down, and carefully stipple it onto the surface of the resin, using a wet brush. Whilst tissue is far more flexible than matting and will thus adopt shapes which matting would doggedly refuse to take, there are limits to its adaptability. If it is necessary to use several pieces of tissue due to the complexity of

The whole of an elaborately contoured facia like the one in this Gordon Keeble GK1 could be moulded from glassfibre — by far the most effective material for the job.

your mould shape, try to position each edge into a high spot on the mould — which means that on the finished item the join will be in shadow.

Once all of the tissue is down on the mould, you can start to lay up a couple of layers of matting. It is advisable to make the first layer 300g matting, followed by a second layer of 450g. Again use the brush as a stipple, and work gently to avoid disturbing the tissue layer.

Grain-effect dash of a TVR race car. Whilst the production cars cosset the occupants in walnut and wilton luxury, racers have to make do with a fundamental facia. It is advisable to install gauges, clocks and other paraphernalia before fitting the dash to the car.

Gently roll out any air bubbles using a paddle or disc roller, and leave the lamination to dry. Wash out your tools, and clean out any excess resin from your pot.

When the initial curing process has happened, excess material can be trimmed off from the edge of the mould using a sharp knife. It will be several hours before the panel can be removed from its mould, by carefully prising apart the edges using first pieces of plastic strip and then strips of hardboard. More than most other laminations, it will probably be necessary to tap over the outside of the mould with a soft-faced mallet as part of the release programme.

All that then will remain will be to wash off the excess dried PVA from the surface of the new moulding using soapy lukewarm water, and to trim off the edges using a sanding disc in your angle grinder. You will find that unlike a conventional moulding, the use of a lay-up resin and tissue as a first coat (as distinct from a gel-coat) has given a soft sheen to the finish, far more akin to a leathercloth trim finish than a high-gloss gel-coat would ever give. If your lamination was so complex that it was necessary to use several pieces of tissue, and for some reason there is a joint prominent, do not despair; remember there are always strips of chromed trim available for covering such joins. If it works for the car manufacturers, it will work for you.

The method of affixing the panel to the vehicle depends entirely on the design of both components; more often than not, colour-keyed self-tapping screws will suffice. Always worth bearing in mind is that it is often easiest to install clocks, switches, and the like in a facia panel before it goes near the car. Using self-tappers rather than a more permanent form of fixing will make any subsequent modifications behind the facia a far easier process than they otherwise might be.

CHAPTER 20

STRENGTHENING GLASSFIBRE PANELS

Time was when most of the bodyshells offered by kit car manufacturers left quite a bit to be desired in terms of quality. It seemed that even when the original formers from which the various moulds had been made were of a high quality, the standard of lamination of copies was less than satisfactory. Fortunately, during the past five years or so, a lot of the manufacturers have realized that in order to exist in an ever-competitive world it is necessary to improve the quality of their output. But even so, there are one or two bodyshells on sale which still need some additional reinforcement, and the same is true of glassfibre replacement panels.

Quite where a panel or bodyshell needs reinforcing is a very subjective matter, as each will be different from the next. Even two successive bodyshells from the same mould can be different, one having adequate strength as it comes, the other needing some form of additional stiffening. As a guide, any large, flat (or flattish) panel will need its basic flat lamination reinforcing, and many bodyshells need some form of stiffening around the scuttle area, to reduce the likelihood of twisting.

Take a bonnet or bootlid from a kit car, with a basic lamination of even thickness throughout, as an example: if you put it on blocks at each corner and can depress the centre by any appreciable amount, it would be worth-

A basic kit car bodyshell outside the Cheetah Cars factory in Newcastle. Whilst Cheetah's Kevin Mason is most particular about his shells being strong, not everybody in the industry is as thorough and some bodies need a little more attention before they can be fitted to the chassis.

while adding some additional stiffening. Start by flatting off the inside of the panel with coarse abrasive paper, having removed any grease which may have got onto the surface between the panel being produced and your taking delivery of it. Now lay strips of paper rope on the panel, attempting to make a cruciform or triangular pattern with them. Cut the lengths so that none overlap each other, and tack them into place on the surface of the lamination by using small blobs of catalysed body filler. Remove any excess filler before the curing process is completed.

Mix up a batch of resin, tinted to the same colour as the rest of the lamination. Cut enough strips of five-inch wide matting to apply two layers over the paper rope. Once the filler has set and the rope is permanently positioned, paint over a coat of catalysed resin, soaking the rope and covering the area several inches either side of the new stiffeners. Start to lay up the matting, using the wet paintbrush as a stipple — using strokes of the brush will succeed only in stretching and separating the matting. Ensure that each piece of mat is thoroughly wet before applying the next piece; any that is still dry will show as smooth and silvery.

Continue the lamination process until all of the rope is covered by two layers of matting, and complete the process by rolling out any air bubbles with a paddle or disc roller. Work from the rope to the edge of the lamination to achieve this most easily. Now wash out your tools, clean out your pot, and leave the resin of your lamination to cure completely. This will take an hour or two, depending upon the prevailing conditions.

As an alternative to paper rope, you could use pieces of timber battening which has had its outer corners radiused. However, this has the disadvantage of a lack of flexibility, and will thus be unsuitable for use on a panel

To ensure torsional rigidity in their bodyshells, TVR add this lateral tube just behind the door shuts. Even though the bulk of the stresses are dealt with by the excellent chassis, TVR consider it necessary to add strength to the body in this way.

which has compound curvatures. The third option is to use pieces of sheet polyurethane foam, which will not only stiffen the structure of the panel, but will also give a good degree of sound insulation, thanks to the absorbent qualities of the foam. This makes this method particularly suitable for use on car bonnets or engine covers.

Start by cutting pieces of foam to the basic shape required, making allowances for the increased depth of the bonnet moulding once the foam has been laminated into place — which means that sufficient clearance should be allowed along the edges of your panel so that it will still shut. Once the basic shape has been cut, make a number of cut-outs in the centre of larger pieces, which will allow the subsequent layers of matting to contact a greater area of the original panel.

The foam can then be affixed to the panel using a catalysed lay-up resin. Once in place, paint over the surface of the foam and the surface of the original panel for a couple of inches around the edges of the foam. Now

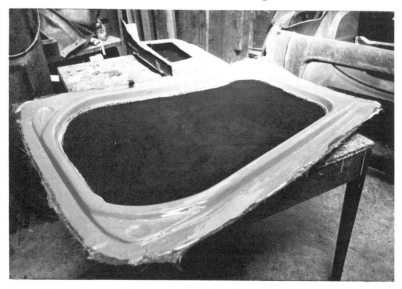

Wherever possible, it pays to add a reinforcing section to the outside edges of opening panels like the bonnet and boot of this Cobra bodyshell.

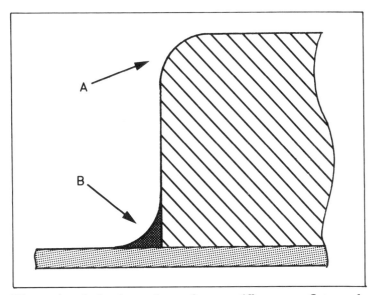

When using timber battening to form a stiffener on a flat panel, round off the corners (A) to facilitate laying the reinforcing lamination over it. The hollow left by the matting at (B) will add strength, if anything, and so need not be filled.

you can start to laminate the foam and bonnet. The foam should have been cut with 45° edges, which will mean that the matting will not be expected to adopt too sharp an angle. Start the lamination process along the edges of the foam, using strips of matting which will run onto the original panel by a couple of inches. Where the matting is on the foam, use a torn edge which can be overlapped by the torn edge of the next piece by an inch or so. Ensure that each piece is completely wetted out before applying the next piece. Continue the process until all of the foam is covered by a layer, and then repeat it so that there is a double layer of matting. It is likely that you will run out of time on a single mix of catalysed resin due to the laborious nature of such a lamination.

Should this occur, you will know about it because the resin will start to go lumpy. Once this happens, roll out the air from whatever matting you have so far put down onto the job, then clean out your pot and tools before

Because of the amount of power that the car will be handling (anything up to 300bhp, depending upon engine fitted) TVR use a complex spaceframe to take the strain, thus leaving the bodyshell relatively stress-free.

making a fresh mix and continuing. On completion of the process, roll out any air bubbles, and leave the lamination to cure completely.

In addition to its use on bonnets, foam can also be used for its sound-proofing properties on bulkheads. Again, there should be a number of cut-outs made in the centre of larger panels of foam, to ensure good adhesion. If two layers of matting are applied to the foam, there will also be a substantial degree of increased rigidity provided by the process. Always remember that it is not the foam which provides stiffening, but the box-section that is formed by the layers of laminate applied over it.

The other main area that I mentioned earlier as being in possible need of stiffening is the scuttle of a complete bodyshell, where the bulkhead meets the outer body panels. This is a problem solved in an entirely different way from those already dealt with.

Earlier in the book (Chapter 8), I mentioned woven rovings, and this is one of those applications for which rovings are perfect. Start by preparing the surface of the inside of the panel area to be reinforced. This is rarely more than a matter of flatting back with coarse abrasive paper to remove any deposits of dust and dirt. It is also most important to remove any grease. Next, cut pieces of woven roving to suit the area to be covered. Aim to cover an area of several inches either side of the corner sections that you are reinforcing. Choose a 2oz roving for this exercise. Woven roving will work quite neatly into an internal bend of up to 90°, once wetted out, but has no provision in its construction for stretch. This means that cuts must be made in pieces which are being applied to a curved surface.

This is far easier done when the roving is dry, so do a 'dummy run' with the various pieces that you will be

Because of the way in which virtually every panel of the GTD 40 is hinged, the areas around the hinges have been laid up to substantially greater thicknesses than the surrounding panels. In this case the hinges are bolted through the panels directly to the spaceframe chassis, to reduce stress on the glassfibre.

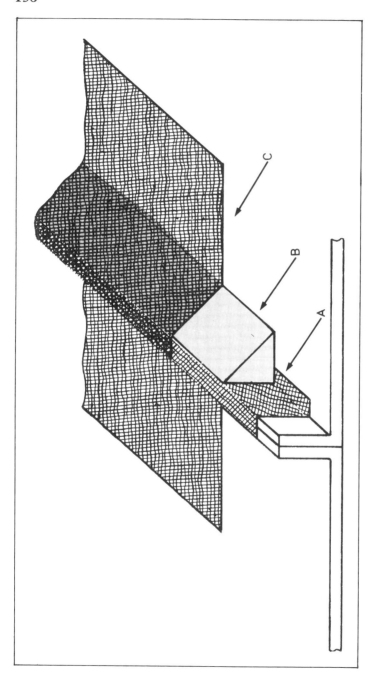

Where two flanges join, they can be substantially reinforced by inserting a piece of foam cut into a wedge shape (B) over the basic wrapover of matting (A) and then adding a further layer of matting (C) over the foam, to a distance of up to six inches from the joint.

applying, making any cuts and then laying the pieces so that you can identify which is destined for where. Once you have prepared the material, you can proceed to tint a batch of lay-up resin. As a guide to quantity, roving takes in about half as much resin again as matting would, so allow about a kilo of resin per square metre of area to be covered for the two layers that you will be applying.

Catalyse the resin, and paint out the area to be laminated. Apply your first piece of roving, and use your brush as a stipple to wet it out thoroughly. The cuts made to accommodate curves will result in either gaps (if you are covering an outside radius) or overlaps (if you are covering an internal radius) which can be attended to subsequently. Roll out any air bubbles after the first layer of roving, and then apply your second layer. Wherever you have made cuts, ensure that those in the second layer of roving are in different places from the first. Should there be any gaps remaining, these can be covered by a strip of roving laid across them. Repeat the rolling out process with your paddle or disc roller until all air bubbles are removed, and ensure that all areas where the roving is pressed into a corner are filled by the lamination. Once you are satisfied with the job, leave it to cure and go and clean off your tools and equipment.

One last area of glass-bodied cars which can require attention at the construction stage is the joining of separate panels into a permanent single structure. Because of mould design techniques, it is highly likely that the two panels will be joined by a flange, and this will have been glassed over with a single piece of matting. The problem here is that there is little support for the join, the flange being expected to bear all of the stress of the two panels. In order to substantially reinforce the area, use pieces of polyurethane foam cut to fit into the corners of the two flange sides. These will hold in place with resin or filler, and can then be permanently affixed by laminating over them with matting and resin. Extend the matting to several inches beyond the foam on each side, and ensure that all air bubbles are removed. Apply two layers of matting to be on the safe side. The angles created by the use of foam will ensure that the matting has not been made to adopt tight angles as it has been laid, and the extent to which they have been overlapped onto the surrounding panels will ensure a far greater area to absorb the panel stresses.

Although sold as brush cleaner, this product can also be used to clean off the back of a lamination prior to adding stiffeners.

CHAPTER 21

METAL PANEL REPAIRS

There are times when it is plainly impractical to make repairs to steel bodywork by patching in pieces of fresh metal; perhaps because of the nature of the damage, or the non-availability of parts, or maybe because you have neither the equipment nor ability to weld in new pieces. Glassfibre is a very useful material in such circumstances, as the process and materials are all within the scope of the average DIY enthusiast.

But there are strict limits to the applicability of glassfibre on metal-bodied machinery. For instance, it would be wholly unsuitable to use as a means of repairing holes in the sill sections of a Ford Escort; this is because the sills are part of the monocoque construction of the vehicle, and thus stress-bearing. Whilst the tensile strength of laminates is a debatable area, you will have a virtually impossible task convincing an MOT tester that your repair is as strong as steel. He will simply raise an eyebrow, and fail the car until you have replaced your laminated repair with a complete new steel panel. Likewise, the inner wings of the same car (and the Escort is merely a typical example, most modern cars are built on the same principle of using a series of panels, interlocked, in place of a separate chassis) cannot be repaired in GRP as they too are stressed components. In fact, many modern cars use both inner and outer wings

With any modern mass-production car such as the Ford Escort series, great care must be taken when using glassfibre — almost all of the body panels are stress-bearing, working as a composite structure instead of a separate chassis.

Controversy has raged for years about the use of one-piece glassfibre replacement front ends for Minis. To be certain that a car so fitted will pass a subsequent MOT test it is necessary to install a tube framework as reinforcement to compensate for the absence of the stiffening provided by the original wing panels.

Photo: Austin Rover.

to form a box-section which is designed to cope with the stresses and strains that would formerly have been dealt with by a chassis independently of the bodyshell. So it is important never to attempt repairs in GRP to a steel panel which was designed as a stress-bearing member.

Having ascertained that you *are* able to execute a repair in glassfibre on a damaged panel, a rust hole in an unstressed area, for example, the first move should be to straighten out any dents or high spots as best you can, using such tools as a hammer or a dent puller. The surface should then be taken right down to bare metal on both sides, for a couple of inches surrounding the area to be repaired. This is easiest to achieve with an angle grinder fitted with a coarse sanding disc. Should you not possess one of these machines, use either a coarse sanding disc attached to an electric drill, or a selection of pieces of coarse abrasive paper wielded by your own fair hands. It is essential that there are no traces of any rust, grease, paint, or anything else foreign on the metal.

Life is made easier if you can remove the panel that you are about to rebuild from the vehicle, as it can then be positioned for the easiest working situation. Unfortunately, this is not always (not often?) a practicality, and in consequence a laminator can find him or herself not only working in an awkward situation, but also attempting to defy gravity.

Whilst resin will adhere to bare metal, it will never bond to it as it would to itself. For that reason, it is worthwhile peppering the area immediately surrounding the hole to be filled with a number of small holes through which the resin can run at the laying-up stage. The size of the holes will vary with their number, but as a guide aim to drill a quarter-inch hole every inch or so around the damage area, about a half-inch outboard of the edge of the damage hole. This will enable the resin to key into the metal far more securely than it would otherwise be able to.

Prepare the materials by tearing yourself enough 450g

matting to cover the hole several times, and tinting a pot of lay-up resin to your desired shade. Catalyse the resin to suit conditions, and apply a paint coat over the bare metal on the inside of the panel to be repaired. Apply your first piece of matting, ensuring that it overlaps the edge of the hole by about an inch and a half. With a small hole, there should be·little problem in wetting out the resin. However, life can be difficult with a large hole — all that will happen is that your brush will displace the centre of the piece of matting. For this reason, most laminators tend to use the trick of pre-wetting their matting. Lay the matting on a piece of clean flat board and wet it out with your brush — as usual, using a stippling action rather than brush strokes to avoid damaging the matting. The piece of wet matting is then placed onto the job, and the edges are tamped down into the waiting paint coat of resin. The process is then repeated until two layers of matting have been applied. That is the job in theory, and it sounds simple. In practice, it can be anything but simple. For a start, the mat will be difficult to roller, and in consequence will probably cure as two separate pieces with a big air bubble between. Then there will be the problem of the wet matting sagging, and eventually drying in the form that it has adopted — which will rarely be that which you have envisaged.

There are a number of tricks which can help here. The first is to use a piece of acetate film to cover the outside of the hole. This is available from any good artists' materials suppliers. Tell them what you are going to use it for, or they will perhaps sell you a particularly good (and thus expensive) acetate that was designed to be used by illustrators. The cheaper the acetate the better, for this particular application. Give this a wax coating, buffed off to a sheen, and tape it into place over the hole to be filled. Now cover that with a sheet of heavy card and tape that into place, too. Acetate and card together make a temporary former to support the wet matting.

If a complete panel can easily be removed (and refitted!), taking it off to work on is far more satisfactory than trying to carry out a repair in situ.

This will allow you to use your paddle roller to remove any air bubbles from between the two layers, and will in turn make for a better bonding process. It will also aid the sticking of the resin to the surrounding metal, and will enable the wet mat to resist the call of gravity.

Another trick is to use a piece of perforated zinc plate, of the type readily available from body repair materials suppliers and from GRP suppliers. This is of great use when the hole to be filled is of an odd compound contour, and cannot easily have acetate placed on its outside. Press the perforated metal into place from behind the hole, and attach it with a couple of self-tapping screws. The mesh can then be shaped close to the exact contours of the panel surface, and laminated over from behind. In this case, the support remains as a permanent part of the repair. Being perforated, the zinc has lots of little holes for resin to seep through and ensure a good bond.

The third method is quite time-consuming, but reasonably worthwhile where neither of the other two tricks will work. This is to make up a former in the shape of the panel by laying strips of glassfibre sheet, made as explained in the first project (see Chapter 15), into place behind the hole, and then laminate over them from behind. As with the zinc plate, the strips can be located by self-tapping screws.

Once the resin has cured and the self-tappers have been removed, you can proceed with the repair. If you used the acetate method, this can be removed, along with its reinforcement card. All three methods will leave you with a rather coarse surface of resined matting, but should the finish be quite smooth it will need roughening by the application of abrasive paper. All that then remains is to build up on your new foundations with body filler, until the area of the repair is flush and undetectable from the surrounding good metal. Spread the filler as smoothly as possible, and keep the surface of it as close to the height of the surrounding metal as

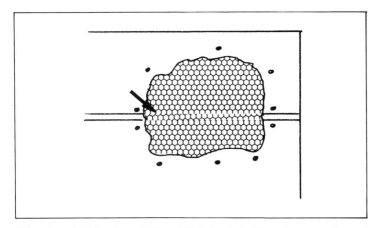

When faced with a large hole to fill, it is advisable to insert a piece of perforated zinc sheet (arrowed) before starting to laminate from behind. This can be located by a number of self-tapping screws which can be removed once the repair is effected.

possible. There is almost invariably a need to apply further, smaller amounts of filler to a repair such as this, due to the tendency for air bubbles to appear as the filler dries. Great patience is called for at this stage of the proceedings to ensure that the surface of the repair is as smooth as the metal which surrounds it. Once you feel satisfied with the quality of your repair work, prime the area with a spray primer, and follow that with a guide coat of matt black paint. Once the paint is dry, sand it back very lightly with 600-grit wet-and-dry paper. Any low or high spots will show immediately, and can be attended to before you apply body colour to the repair. Tiny airholes (the size of a pinhead, but no bigger) can be treated with a stopper paste, available wherever you obtain your filler.

One great use for glassfibre laminate repairs on a steel-bodied car is fixing door sections which have rusted away. These are rarely noticed until it is too late to do much about them with conventional body repair techniques, as by the time the damage is spotted the inner section of the door has separated itself from the outer skin. Once again, a glassfibre repair job can save the day.

Whilst a substantial number of the panels on this Metro 6R4 are laminates, they are supported by a tubular metal spaceframe — and thus bear little stress. This car also indicates the versatility of lamination; trying to create such shapes from sheet metal would be extremely difficult, and the weight penalties would be great.

Photo: Austin Rover.

As with repairing a hole in a panel, life is made much easier by removing the offending door from the car. Turn the door upside-down, and remove all traces of rust, paint and so forth from the rotten area, and from the surrounding metal. There is a distinct possibility that the inner and outer parts of the door will need to be realigned, so use a pair of clamps for this purpose. It is worthwhile cutting a couple of blocks of wood to the thickness of the door's inner section and placing them inside the frame, to avoid the clamps drawing the two parts too close together.

If, as so often happens, the bottom of the door has disappeared completely, make up a replacement strip to cover the hole. This can be from more or less any materials you can find handy, though aluminium sheet and cardboard are the two most suitable. At the time of fitting this, stuff a handful of old rags into the door frame to protect the window winder and lock mechanisms from dripping resin. Mix up a batch of resin (about 500g should be about right for the average door) with what ever pigment tint you desire, catalyse it, and paint over the area of bare metal that you have cleared, together with the strip which covers the worst of the hole. Lay up a number of strips of surfacing tissue, each overlapping the previous one, until the whole of the resin is covered. Ensure that the tissue is well saturated and pressed into the corners (as previously, use the brush as a stipple) before proceeding with the next stage, which is to reinforce the tissue with two layers of 300g matting. As with any lamination job, run off the open edge of the door frame with both tissue and matting to ensure adequate coverage of the laminate. Once the lamination process is complete, remove any air bubbles with a disc roller, taking special care with the corners. Clean out your tools, and leave the resined door to dry.

Once the initial curing period has been reached, the excess material which has overlapped the edge of the door can be removed with a sharp knife. Several hours

Inserting a new section into a steel panel can result in an indistinguishable repair if enough attention to quality is paid at the filling and finishing stage.

later, when the resin has cured completely, you can sand down the surface of the matting to a smooth finish which can be painted. Whilst such a repair will almost always show, it is undoubtedly cheaper than purchasing a complete new door — if you are bothered about the finish, you could always tidy it up further by applying an outer layer of surfacing tissue once the matting has been laminated into place. The only real limiting factor on the quality of the result you can obtain is your time and patience.

A third area where glassfibre lamination is used as a repair on metal-bodied motor cars is the floor. As explained in the first part of this chapter in relation to holes in outer panels, great care must be taken to ensure that you are not dealing with a structural member — on some cars the floor is stressed, whilst on others it isn't. It is advisable to seek the advice of a local MOT tester before proceeding, particularly if a large area of the floor is involved.

Having established that you can safely make a repair without affecting the strength of the floor, the process can commence with the removal of all traces of paint, rust, and so forth from the hole edges, to an area of several inches outwards. Next, drill a series of quarter-inch holes every inch or so apart, an inch out from the edge of the hole. These will serve to help the lamination to bond more solidly to the metalwork. Make up a piece of flat glassfibre sheet with two layers of 300g matting as per an earlier project (Chapter 15), but without using an initial gel-coat — use a lay-up resin throughout, so that the subsequent surface of the sheet is infiltrated by the matting.

Cut a piece of your sheet so that it fills the hole in the floor, and score lines into both sides of the sheet with your angle grinder. This will give the resin more of a key. Locate the insert piece, and hold it into place by taping it from below. Mix up a batch of resin and catalyst, and paint over the insert and the surrounding bare metal.

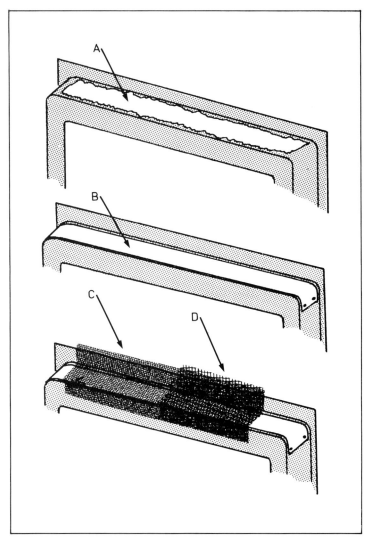

One of the major applications for glassfibre on monocoque cars is repairing the bottoms of doors which have fallen prey to the dreaded rust-bug. Start by cleaning off the edges (A) to remove all traces of rust and flaking material. A strip of aluminium or card (B) should then be affixed to cover the hole and provide a basis onto which the matting can be laminated. Start by applying a layer of tissue (C) and follow that with a layer or two of matting (D). Wrap the laminate around the end of the door, to ensure a good bond. Also overlap the edge of the door — the excess can be removed once cured.

Onto this, lay a piece of pre-cut matting and wet it out completely, using your brush as a stipple. Lay a second piece of matting on top of the first, and roll out any air bubbles. The lamination can now be left to dry whilst you clean out your tools and equipment.

Once the resin has cured completely, use your angle grinder to remove any drips of resin from the underside of the car, and wipe down the surface with a rag damped in acetone to remove any dust. Mix up a small amount of resin and catalyst, and paint over the whole of the prepared area beneath the car. Wet out a single layer of matting on a piece of board, and take this to the job. Affix it by first stippling it with your brush, and then rolling it out with a paddle roller to remove any air bubbles. Because you are defying gravity, you will need to revisit the piece several times during the next few minutes, so keep your roller handy ready to use it as necessary. Once the resin has cured, you will have a permanent and durable repair which can be painted over to match the surrounding bodywork.

CHAPTER 22

GLASSFIBRE PANEL REPAIRS

Even though it does not rust away, and is surprisingly resilient to minor knocks and abrasions, glassfibre falls some way short of being totally bulletproof and thus needs to be repaired from time to time.

One of the first problems that comes to light is the outer surface of a bodyshell, the gel-coat, cracking and crazing. There may be any of a dozen causes to blame for this happening, such as something heavy being dropped onto a panel, a part of the bodyshell being hit by a parking car (or by a bollard jumping out at the car, if some insurance claims are to be believed), a stone chip, undue stress around a door lock or boot hinge, or even excessive body flexing.

In order to treat the problem correctly, it is essential to appreciate what has caused the particular crack and then take steps to ensure that it won't recur. For instance, if you are dealing with a series of crazing lines around a door handle, you can be almost certain that the reason is too much flexing in the immediate vicinity of the handle. Likewise, it could be that the little, sporadic bursts of crazing that decorate your front wings are down to stone chips being thrown up by the road wheels against the underside of the laminate.

Should you find that your particular problem is ascribable to a door or boot handle flexing, the first part of the repair should be to reinforce the area behind the handle or lock mechanism, not only so that it is stronger but also to increase the area absorbing the load. To do this, first sand back the inside surface of the laminate to remove all traces of grease and dust, and then mix a batch of resin and catalyst. Apply a paint coat of resin to the prepared surface, and onto this lay up either two layers of 300g matting, or one layer of 600g woven roving. Aim to cover an area six inches around the lock handle mechanism. Where the handle is close to a panel edge, try to wrap the matting or roving into the corner, so that the surfaces are sharing the loading on the lock handle. Once you have laid your matting, which should be applied with the brush used end-on as a stipple to avoid stretching the material, and are sure that it is thoroughly wetted-out, roller out any air bubbles with a paddle or disc roller, and leave the lamination to cure whilst you clean out your brushes.

Once the new lamination has cured, you can start to attend to the surface crazing by using a grinder to take all of the crazes back to good glassfibre, just as you would take surface rusting back to bare metal on a steel panel. Try to avoid being over-zealous, and just take the cracks back as far as necessary. At the edges of the area you have been grinding away, aim to feather the surface gradually back to the correct height — this will help to avoid the possible tell-tale signs of a repair at a later date.

It is unlikely that you will have gone much below 0.025in (0.6mm) down into the surface of the laminate in order to remove all traces of cracked gel-coat. To build this back up to the surface, you will need a small amount of catalysed lay-up resin, a piece of tissue cut to the shape of the indentation but slightly undersized, and a portion of body filler. Brush a layer of lay-up resin onto the surface of the indentation, and stipple your piece of tissue onto this until it is quite flat and thoroughly wetted through with resin. Take great care to remove all traces of air from beneath your tissue — stippling in the tissue from the centre of the piece outwards to the edges will generally sort this out.

Once the resin has cured completely, the surface should be skimmed with a thin spreading of catalysed filler and left to cure. This can then be sanded smooth, starting with a coarse abrasive paper (60-grit, or thereabouts) and finishing with a fine one. Inspect the area closely for air bubbles in the filler surface, and repeat the process of skimming the filler on and rubbing it down once cured until you are satisfied that the surface is as smooth as that around it. To be certain that the eventual repair will be undetectable, spray the repair with primer, following that with a light coat of black paint. Once the paint is dry, lightly dust over the repair with a piece of 600-grit abrasive paper and any low or high spots, and any air bubbles, will show up. Any tiny air bubbles are best dealt with by using a stopping compound, which is readily available from wherever you buy your filler.

Once you are satisfied with your repair, the holes for the handle and fixing screws can be redrilled, and the hardware refitted. Take great care to ensure that your holes are large enough, too; a surprising number of cracks are down to the bolts being forced through too-tight holes, which unduly stresses the immediate area.

The same principles of repair apply for crazing around the base of a windscreen, which is another common problem on GRP-bodied machines. These marks are caused by the GRP being allowed to flex, whereas the glass obviously will not. Further, the glass is also quite a heavy material to carry. To execute a repair, remove the windscreen, clean up the area behind the crazing, and reinforce it by laminating in several layers of 450g matting before continuing to treat the surface damage as previously explained. Only when the repair is complete should the screen be refitted. In some cases I have known, the size of the aperture for the screen has been to blame for the subsequent bodywork problems, as it has been very slightly undersized. This has meant that the windscreen sealing rubber has been compressed slightly more than it ought to be, and has thus been unable to absorb any of the flexing that it has been designed to cope with. What has then happened is that the strain has been passed straight onto the surrounding laminated frame. Shaving as little as a couple of millimetres from the frame has been enough to prevent a recurrence of crazing.

Where the problem has been traced directly to stones flying up from the wheels and hitting the underside of a wing, the best way to deal with the problem is first to repair the damage as previously described, and to then make up a set of wheelarch liner panels from glassfibre. These can be cut out of cardboard and taped into place, and then laminated over with a single layer of matting. Once the laminate has cured properly, the assemblies can then be removed from the car, and reinforced by the addition of a further layer of matting on either side of the former. Once the resin has cured, the inserts can be trimmed and affixed to the car using self-tapping screws into the inner wings, chassis, or whatever other convenient point you are able to find.

By affixing them in this manner, they can be readily removed for maintenance purposes, but when in place will act as a barrier to any flying stones or other debris. As they are going under the car, it would make sense to pre-tint the lay-up resin in black.

Moving on from crazing and starring of the gel-coat, the next problem to deal with is the crack. Whenever a panel has been the victim of a parking injury or whatever, the chances are that the complete laminate will have broken right through. The first part of your repair should be to remove all trim pieces from the area (this should be done with any kind of repair — failure to do so is nothing short of laziness, a degree of sloppiness which will show in the finished result) and to then clean up the edges of the crack by running your angle grinder through the inside of it. Once all loose bits of material have been cleared away, sand back the back of the panel from the inside to remove all traces of dust, grease and paint.

Cut enough 450g matting to cover the area of the crack, and a couple of inches all around it. Mix up a batch of tinted lay-up resin to the shade of the bodyshell, and catalyse it. Apply a paint coat of resin to the area that you have prepared on the back of the panel, and apply your two layers of matting, ensuring that they are completely wetted-out and free of air bubbles (rolling

The way to deal with a crack is to start by removing any damaged material from the crack itself with a cutting disc.

them out as necessary with a paddle roller) before leaving the lamination to cure properly.

Once the resin has cured properly, it is a simple matter of finishing off the repair by building up the level of the crack to that of the surrounding surface with filler, and rubbing it back. As with the previous repair involving

The two sides of the crack can then be joined together with a set of cleats. Whilst self-tapping screws at the points arrowed are the most common way of affixing the cleats, some laminators now use a glue gun — the glue can be removed from the gel-coat surface without difficulty.

A glue gun in action. The adhesive itself is inadequate for permanent bonding of glassfibre panels — which makes it ideal for affixing temporary cleats.

filler, it is advisable to apply a guide coat of black paint as a means of ensuring that the eventual repair will be undetectable.

Which brings us neatly to the next type of repair, reassembling a panel which has had a shade more damage — to the point where it is in lots of little pieces. The key here is to collect all the pieces at the time of the incident, and to rebuild them on the car. Larger pieces can be held into place on the bodyshell by making jointing cleats from strips of glassfibre sheet. A self-tapping screw at each end of the strip will enable you to affix two pieces together. Smaller pieces can be positioned by taping them into place. In either case, the (temporary) fixings should be on the outside of the moulding. Whatever the size of the piece, it is advisable to clean off the edges back to solid laminate — otherwise, you are not guaranteed a secure join, and you may well find air bubbles within the subsequent repair.

Once you have the various parts of the panel reassembled, clean off the back of the panel with your angle grinder and set them into place by laying up a single lamination of 450g matting and resin on the back of the panel. When this has set, you can start the repair process in earnest.

Remove all of the cleats and tape that were holding the various pieces into place. If you were both careful and lucky, the various parts should all be at roughly the same height as the surrounding panel. If they are not, don't worry too much as they can be brought into alignment without too much difficulty.

Clean out the various cracks in the panel, using your angle grinder to leave 45° angles to all the edges. As it is quite likely that your holding piece of matting will have suffered from the onslaught of the grinder, lay up another layer or two of matting, extended to something like three inches around the area of the original damage. Once the resin has cured properly, use a mix of body filler to bring the level of the cracks up to that of the panelwork. This can be sanded to shape using a selection of abrasive papers, starting with coarse 40-grit and finishing with 600-grit. On a body panel, it is advisable to use your paper wrapped around a block, to avoid creating ruts with the pressure of your fingers through the paper.

Any of the inserted pieces which are slightly mis-placed will soon show as proud or low of the surrounding panel. Low spots can be brought up to the height of the rest of the surrounding area by roughing off the surface, laying in a piece of tissue, and laminating it into place with lay-up resin, following it with body filler once cured — in just the same way as gel cracks were dealt with earlier. High spots should receive the same treat-ment, once their surface has been taken down with the angle grinder.

This is a very laborious process, and consumes a great amount of time and patience. However, if you stick with it you can execute an effective repair to even the most badly damaged of panels. As with the previous illus-trations of repairs using filler, it is strongly advised that you make use of the guide coat over primer technique before applying a coat of colour to the repair.

Where the gaps between pieces of a panel to be repaired are particularly wide, it would be asking rather a lot of the filler to stay together for a long period — cracking almost always results from prolonged use. Instead, fill the cracks up with a catalysed mix of loose chopped strand glassfibre and resin (available ready-to-use from Strand Glassfibre) to just below the surface height of the panel, and then skim it with filler to finish off. This will give a degree of strength greater than filler alone.

Should you be in the unfortunate position of being unable to get the various parts which once filled a hole in your panel, the task of executing a repair becomes more complex. It may be that you know the whereabouts of the original moulds for your car, in which case you are

As you can see, the cleats have brought the two sides of the piece being repaired into perfect alignment.

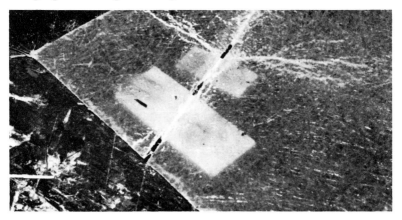

The back of the piece to be repaired. Two layers of matting laminated into place properly will see to it that this piece won't crack again. Extend the repair patches to a couple of inches either side of the crack.

probably best advised to contact the owners, detailing the extent of damage to your machine, and asking them to produce a repair section which covers the hole and the area surrounding it. Then it is a simple matter of cutting out the edges of the hole to a tidy shape, cutting out your repair section to suit, and mating the two together. Hold them in place with a selection of cleats made from GRP sheet, laminate two layers of matting from behind, and treat exactly as though you had got all of the pieces in the first place.

Should the whereabouts of the original mould be unknown to you, it is worthwhile contacting the owners' club for your car, should there be one. That way you could either find out that someone, somewhere has some moulds, or somebody is prepared to allow you to use their own car from which to spring a mould which will in turn enable you to produce a repair panel of your own.

Or you could be unlucky and be the sole owner of a one-off car, the moulds for which have long-since disappeared. In that case, all that you can do is to execute a scratch repair. Start by cleaning up the area of damage, removing all traces of foreign material from the back of the moulding, and all loose particles from the edges of the hole. To give your lamination something to cling to which will follow the contours of the panel to a reasonable degree, affix a piece of perforated zinc sheet to the back of the panel using self-tapping screws. The zinc should be very slightly oversized for the hole. Arrange the metal so that it is as close to the shape of the panel as you can manage, and laminate it into place from behind, with two layers of 300g matting and enough resin to ensure that it is wetted out. Remove all air bubbles from the matting, and ensure that the lamination extends at least two inches onto the bodywork all round the hole.

Once the laminate has cured, the self-tapping screws can be removed and you can start work on the front of the panel. Firstly, remove any over-long drips of resin which have oozed through the perforated metal, using your angle grinder. Cut a piece of 300g matting to the exact shape of the hole that you are filling, but very slightly undersize. Mix a small pot of resin and catalyst, and paint over the metal. Stipple on the piece of matting, ensuring that it is perfectly located and completely wetted out — any dry areas will show as silvery and shiny. Ensure that there are no air bubbles present.

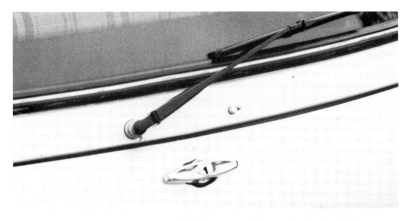

By laying up an extra couple of thicknesses of matting behind the lock mechanism on this Mini bootlid when I copied it in glassfibre, I avoided the possibility of its cracking at a later date.

Leave the resin to cure, and wash out your tools.

Once the job is dry, you can complete the repair by building up the surface with filler and sanding it down to shape. As previously, work methodically and make regular inspections for airholes in the surface of the filler. Finish the repair with a guide coat of black paint over the primer to be certain of a good surface before top coating.

Whilst all of the above methods refer to holes in a panel, the same principles are adopted for larger repairs, such as accident damage to a corner of the car. The key to successful repairs in this area is to know when to repair or when to replace; it can take several times as long, and cost as much in materials, to execute a complicated repair to a damaged corner as it would to simply cut off the damaged area and attach a replacement section. Most of the manufacturers of GRP-bodied cars, whether their product is sold as a kit or as a ready-to-drive showroom car, supply repair sections. Contact the manufacturer before going anywhere near your car with an electric saw or angle grinder.

To affix a repair panel, start by cutting off the damaged area to suit the new section, and clean off the

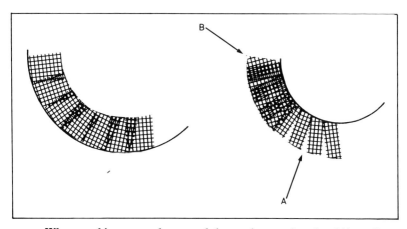

When working around a curved shape, the matting should be split so that it will overlap in the case of an inside radius (left). Round an outside radius (right), the gaps left in the first layer (A) can be covered by the second layer (B).

area six inches or so back from the edge on the inside of the bodywork. Locate the new section, and hold it into place with a number of cleats made from GRP sheet. Use a tape measure to ensure that the new section is square to the rest of the bodywork, and in exactly the right position. This is not really a job to attempt single-handed — enlist the aid of a competent friend.

Once in position, the new section can be permanently affixed to the rest of the car by laminating strips of matting across the back of the joint. Apply at least three layers of 450g matting, ensuring that each piece is thoroughly wetted-out before proceeding to lay on the next piece. Run the matting a distance of five or six inches either side of the join to ensure a strong bond. Roll out the new lamination throughout to ensure that there are no air bubbles present.

After the resin has cured completely, the repair can be finished by using filler to build up the cracks where the two sections join, and also to stop the holes left by the self-tapping screws which had held the cleats in place whilst the joining process was being executed.

PART 4

APPENDICES

APPENDIX 1

LAMINATING FAULTS

1: GEL-COAT

Problem	Cause	Remedy
Wrinkled finish:	*Gel-coat too thin:*	Ensure adequate coverage.
	Matting laid before gel coat has cured:	Allow sufficient curing time.
	Over-slow curing:	Increase catalyst or ambient temperature.
Pinholes on surface:	*Contamination by acetone from brush:*	Ensure brush is completely dry before starting.
	Aeration of gel:	Stir less vigorously next time you mix a batch.
	Moisture on mould:	Ensure everything is completely clean and dry.
Bubbles on surface:	*Gel-coat too thick:*	Ensure even thin coverage.
	Moisture in resin:	Ensure resin is pure.
Patchy colouring:	*Poor mixing:*	Mix thoroughly.
	Uneven gel-coat:	Ensure even, thin coverage.
Streaks in colour:	*Contaminated gel:*	Ensure resin and pot are pure and clean.

Gel not curing:	*Not catalysed:*	Clean mould and re-gel with catalysed mix.
	Too little catalyst or too cool workshop:	Increase amount of MEKP to maximum 3%. Heat premises properly.
Gel not spreading on mould surface:	*Wrong release agent:*	Clean off mould and apply adequate correct release agents.

2: LAY-UP RESIN & MATTING

Problem	Cause	Remedy
Bubbles in laminate:	*Air not rolled out from job when laying up matting:*	Roll out lamination thoroughly with paddle or disc roller.
	Moisture in resin:	Ensure materials and workshop are completely dry at all times.
Lamination breaking up:	*Matting not wetted-out properly:*	Wet out thoroughly.
	Matting damp:	Keep in dry place.
	Grease contamination:	Wipe area down with acetone.
	Resin not catalysed:	Start afresh with correct amount of MEKP.
Porous lamination:	*Matting too dry:*	Wet out thoroughly.

3: LAMINATION DIFFICULTIES

Problem	Cause	Remedy
Gel not releasing from mould:	*Insufficient or wrong release agent:*	Use plenty of correct release agent.
	Lamination not cured completely:	Leave in mould until completely cured.
	Excessive force with removal aids:	Be more gentle.

Laminate not adhering to gel-coat:	*Wrong lay-up resin for gel-coat, or vice versa:*	Ensure both resins are compatible.
Mat pattern showing through gel-coat:	*Laminate laid up before gel-coat has cured completely:*	Allow gel-coat to cure completely.
Stiffening rib lines showing through gel:	*Stiffeners added before first mat layers have cured completely:*	Allow longer between processes.

This is a list of the general problems that are encountered during lamination. There is one other which often seems to be overlooked, and that is when, despite the conditions being right and the catalyst being added to resin in the correct proportions, it still takes an awfully long time before the laminate will cure (if at all). This is almost always down to the age of the materials being used; resin has a limited shelf-life and so must be used within a reasonable period of time if success is to be achieved. If you are at all in doubt about the age of the resin on your workshop shelf, try out a small amount before attempting the job you have in mind. If the resin doesn't behave as it ought, replace it with fresh stock. For the amateur laminator who will undertake one job every few months, it makes most sense to buy whatever materials are needed fresh each time. The discounts that can be gained by buying in bulk are worthless if half the quantity has to be thrown out at a later date.

APPENDIX 2

GLASSFIBRE TERMINOLOGY

Accelerator: Substance added to resin to increase its drying time, once catalysed.

Acetone: Solvent for resin.

Barrier cream: Skin cream used to protect the skin from harmful substances, and to make subsequent washing easier.

Binder: Slightly adhesive substance added to glassfibre strands when making them into matting.

Catalyst: Normally methyl ethyl ketone peroxide (MEKP), which reacts with accelerator to generate heat within resin — the heat which leads to the resin curing.

Chopped strand: Short pieces of glassfibre strand.

Close woven: Fabric made from glassfibre strand which is of very close construction.

Core: Spacing pieces of material between two internal sides of a lamination.

Cracking: Break in lamination which goes right through construction.

Crazing: Breaking up of gel-coat, where lamination is left intact behind it.

Curing: Process of resin changing from liquid to solid state.

Curing time: Elapsed time between adding the catalyst and the resin being hard.

Feathering: Progressively working through a surface

so that the edge forms a gradual slope.

Fibreglass: Trade mark of Pilkington Glass for their glassfibre products.

Filler: Resin combined with another material (usually French chalk) to make a dough-like, pliable mixture for filling spaces.

Foam: Plastic-based material which traps air in tiny bubbles. Very light and reasonably durable.

Gel: Jelly-like resin used to provide a hard, glazed finish to a lamination.

Glassfibre: What this book is all about. Seriously though, glassfibre is the finely-stranded, spun glass which is made into matting, roving, and so forth. When combined with cured resin it makes an extremely strong laminate.

GRP: Glassfibre-reinforced plastic. The combination of glassfibre and cured resin, which is a form of plastic.

Hardener: Catalyst.

Laminate: Combination of glassfibre matting, roving or whatever, with cured resin.

Laying-up: Progressive building of a lamination, layer by layer.

Mould: Former into which a lamination is laid up.

Moulding: Product of above operation.

Open weave: Glassfibre cloth or matting with lots of space between strands.

Plain weave: Standard cloth, similar in appearance to clothing fabrics.

Plastic: Product group of petroleum by-products, among which resin for glassfibre lamination is found.

Putty: Though sometimes used to describe filler mix, this is not strictly accurate; putty has a more pliable make-up.

Release agent: Any substance which is applied to a mould surface to enable a subsequent lamination an easy release.

Resin: Liquidized plastic which sets to a solid, brittle state when catalysed.

Roving: Continuous strands of spun glassfibre. Can be either continuing thread for wrapping, or woven into cloth. Immense strength when laminated with resin.

Sandwich: Term given in this context to a core material surrounded on either side by sheets of laminate.

Styrene: Liquid of plastics family used as a thinning agent for resins.

Tacky: In this instance, retaining a stickiness when touched. Can also be used to describe a particularly bad-taste one-off construction attached to a car . . .

Thixotropic: Liquid which is thick, and will not flow easily when poured.

Unidirectional: Laid in one direction.

Viscosity: Measure of the flow capability of a liquid.

Woven: Systematic laying of strands of fibre to create a cloth so that each successive row interlocks with the rest of those already laid.

One of the chain of Strand Glassfibre stores throughout Great Britain, a one-stop shop for all DIY glassfibre materials and equipment.

APPENDIX 3

USEFUL ADDRESSES

Wherever you experience difficulty in obtaining a product locally, contact the address below for details of their nearest agent, branch or stockist.

Bighead Bonding Fasteners
Unit 15
Elliott Road
West Howe Industrial Estate
BOURNEMOUTH
Dorset BH11 8LZ
01202 574601
(Threaded bonding fasteners)

British Industrial Plastics
Popes Lane
Oldbury
WARLEY
W Midlands B69 4PD
0121 544 1555
(BIP Beetle resins)

Farecla Products Limited
Broadmeads, WARE
Herts SG12 9PY
01920 465041
(Polishing and finishing products)

Llewellyn Ryland Limited
Haden Street
BIRMINGHAM
W Midlands B12 9DB
0121 440 2284
(Pigment tints)

Protex Fasteners Limited
Arrow Road
REDDITCH
Worcestershire B98 8PA
01527 63231
(Latches and handles)

Strand Glassfibre Limited
Williams Way
Hinkwick Road
Wollaston
WELLINGBOROUGH
Northants
01933 664455
(All glassfibre products)